United Way of Lane County

PROJECT IMPACT REPORTS

United Way of Lane County

Oregon Community Programs

Be YOUR BEST

BURRITO BRIGADE
We Rise By Lifting Others

Oregon
Family Support
Network

dia*
dialogues in action

Dialogues In Action
408 NW 12th Ave, Suite 506
Portland, OR 97209
503.329.4816
dialoguesinaction.com

CONTENTS

Foreword

Lane County is blessed with a robust and diverse nonprofit sector: organizations and individuals working hard every day to deliver critical services to improve lives in our community. As a United Way, we are honored to serve as a bridge and connector between the passion of donors and volunteers, and the mission-driven organizations that we partner with. Over the last two years alone, we have supported over 150 community-based organizations from across the county – from Florence to McKenzie Bridge, Junction City, Springfield, Eugene, and Cottage Grove – with responsive and strategic grant awards and programmatic partnerships.

We know our partners do good work but developing the capacity to understand and evaluate the impact of programs – getting beyond "counting widgets" – can be a challenging endeavor. Partnering with Dialogues in Action has been a powerful opportunity for us to provide grantees with the tools and framework they need "to prove and improve" their impact. The organizations that share their findings in this book have been persistent, curious, self-reflective, and did a lot of hard work to produce the results you'll see here. We are proud of and grateful to the more than ten organizations that have participated in Project Impact cohorts in Lane County since 2019. Together, these organizations are helping shape the culture of our nonprofit sector in Lane County: leading by example to elevate the importance of substantive impact evaluation.

Introduction to the Project

The aim of Project Impact is to develop in nonprofits the ability to do credible self-studies of their impact.[1] As such, this is a capacity-building project. The reports in this compendium are written by the nonprofit teams and represent the findings from their data collection and analysis.

This project follows the traditions of participatory evaluation. In a participatory evaluation approach, those who are doing the work also become the evaluators of the effects of the work. This requires capacity-building for the teams, for a self-study form of evaluation requires the development of skills, theoretical understanding, practice in the techniques, and attention to fidelity of implementation in order to ensure the proper level of rigor.

The development of evaluation capacity takes time and iteration. It requires both instruction and practice – training in some of the leading techniques of research accompanied by ongoing applications and practice. This project recognizes the power of partnership, the enrichment

---

1 This project is primarily focused on developing the ability of staff teams to implements self-studies about the effects of their programs. It is not designed to provide an experimental or quasi-experimental version of impact evaluation. Instead, it is an effort to upgrade the existing capability of each organization and give them tools to gather data on the attributed impact both qualitatively and quantitatively from the subjects they serve.

of cross-pollination of ideas among like-minded organizations, the durable impact of a learning community, and the potential inspiration for a sector when exemplars are developed and elevated.

Project Impact takes teams of leaders from nonprofits through a process of discovery about the power of evaluation. The idea is to develop the ability to see and communicate the effects of the programs on the people they are designed to serve. There are three primary movements to the project: (1) Intended impact, (2) Inquiry, and (3) Implication.

Project Design

The project begins with a focus on the work of identifying and clarifying the intended impact of each of the participating programs. Once the ideas have been developed and indicators identified, the teams then design a questionnaire to collect data about quantitative measures and a qualitative interview protocol to collect qualitative data. These data are analyzed. Themes are identified and then translated into findings. From the findings, the teams develop program responses and communiques of their impact.

The fundamental elements of the Project Impact follow an arc of evaluation design:

Part 1 - Intended Impact

This project begins with the identification and clarification of what effects are intended through the work of each of the projects. Each team develops an articulation of intended impact to include the components necessary for evaluation design.

A. Main Ideas of Impact

Each team identifies and crafts ideas of impact to frame the intention of direct impact for the program. In some cases, these ideas are mapped in relation to the secondary and tertiary impacts of the program to gain clarity about the fundamental notions of desired effect as a direct consequence of the program or service rendered.

B. "What We Mean"

From these primary ideas, the teams then develop a brief explication of the meaning of their ideas of impact. This translates ideas that are occasionally technical and into messages accessible to all.

C. Quantitative Indicators

Teams then identify Quantitative indicators for each of the ideas. The aim is to generate five or six of the most critical indicators for each idea, paying attention to the data power, proxy power, and communication power of each of the key ideas. As well, the intent in this step is to identify a range of cognitive, affective, and behavioral indicators that can be measured through metrics.

D. Qualitative Indicators

Teams also identify qualitative indicators in this stage. These indicators are articulations of the structural and qualitative elements of growth and development that signal progress toward key ideas of impact. The qualitative indicators become the basis for the protocol construction to inform the in-depth interviews in the inquiry phase.

This section of the project leads each team to develop a clear theory of change, including the outcomes, indicators, and principles embedded in the particular approach that is implemented by each team.

Part 2 - Inquiry

In the inquiry stage of the project, each team designs and implements a strategy for data gathering. These take two forms: a questionnaire to collect quantitative data and an in-depth interview to gather qualitative data.

A. Quantitative Data and Analysis

For each of the quantitative indicators, teams construct items for a questionnaire. Since these projects are not intended to provide experimental or quasi-experimental inquiry, the attribution of effect is built into the questionnaire items. The questionnaire is deployed, in most cases, to the entire population of recipients the program reaches. Data are analyzed mostly using measures of central tendency. The teams then design displays of the data and narrative for their report.

B. Qualitative Data and Analysis

The development of a qualitative design encompasses a number of steps, including the following:

1. Protocol Design. Each team designs an in-depth interview protocol that uses the *Heart Triangle*™ method of question design. These produces a protocol of about nine sequences of questions (18 questions in total) to be used as a guide for seeking data about the awareness and reflection of subjects' structural shifts and developments of growth and progress.

2. Sample. Each team identifies a sample of subjects using a purposeful stratified technique to identify a selection representative of the population being served.

3. Data Collection. Interviews are convened, most lasting between 45 minutes and 1 hour in length. Data are collected via notes during the interview, and then augmented immediately following the interview to provide a substantive rendering of the interview.

4. Data Analysis. Team members apply a four-step model of analysis to each of the interviews. This process provides them with an accessible version of analysis and interpretation to illuminate the primary themes from each interview. While the process is accessible, working through the data from each interview four times using different lenses of analysis each time provides a rigor to the analytical process that yields insight far beyond what is overt and obvious in the data.

5. Thematics. Through a guided and facilitative process, the entire data corpus is then examined. Themes are mapped through meta-analysis of the emerging insights.

6. Findings. The teams then examine each of the themes to discover and communicate the findings. These are rendered with explanation, illustration from the raw data, and significance.

Part 3 - Implications

The intent of the project is not to leave teams simply with a report about their program's effects, but rather to use the insights from the evaluation to guide the further development of the program. This takes two forms:

A. Program Adjustments

The team then takes each of the findings from the evaluation and considers possible program adjustments informed by the discoveries of the evaluation. This keeps the evaluation relevant for program application and improvement.

B. Program Experiments

In addition, the teams work to identify potential design experiments that they might run as an implication of the insights gained through the evaluation.

In this stage, the teams also begin to develop a report of the evaluation findings as well as other possible communiques of their discoveries to staff, stakeholders, funders, and other members of the community.

The Reports

The reports from the organizations in this cohort are included in the following compendium. These include highlights from the three movements of Project Impact. For each participating organization, there is an explication of the primary findings from the evaluation accompanied by the programmatic responses of strategy and design. Since each organization has unique strategy and ethos, each report exhibits unique character and personality. Each report also includes both "prove" findings (evidence of impacts being achieved) and "improve" findings (areas for attention and further development). These reports are windows into the effects of the work of these organizations in the lives of the people they serve.

Oregon Community Programs

Treatment Foster Parents

Ana Day, Kym Broten, Nicolle Kuhn, Alice Wheeler, Jaimie Broadhead

Organization and Program Overview

Oregon Community Programs (OCP) is a private nonprofit agency that provides research-based treatment and prevention services to children and families. Since 2001, OCP has provided a range of OHP-funded, evidence-based practices to the families of Lane County and the State of Oregon, with particular expertise in serving foster children and families. Each year we serve approximately 400 youth and families in our programs, primarily in Lane County.

OCP hosted many of the initial randomized controlled trials for Treatment Foster Care Oregon (TFCO). TFCO is the only treatment foster care intervention that meets the highest level of empirical validation[1]. OCP contracts with Oregon Youth Authority (OYA) and the Oregon Department of Human Services (ODHS) to deliver treatment foster care services to up to 40 youth in homes that are trained and supported to deliver TFCO to fidelity.

TFCO, formerly known as Multidimensional Treatment Foster Care (MTFC) was developed in 1983 by Dr. Patricia Chamberlain, PhD, Senior Research Scientist at the Oregon Social Learning Center. TFCO has been found to be an effective evidence-based treatment

---

[1] https://www.blueprintsprograms.org/factsheet/treatment-foster-care-oregon

model[2] and has received numerous awards and recognitions, including being designated as a national Blueprints Model Program, a Center for Substance Abuse Prevention Exemplary Program for Strengthening America's Families, and a U.S. Department of Education Exemplary Program for Safe, Disciplined, and Drug-Free Schools. For further information on TFCO, *www.tfcoregon.com*

Intended Impact

As a result of their participation in OCP's TFCO program, we hope that:

- ◆ **Treatment foster parents feel fulfilled, capable, and confident in their roles.** Foster parents are committed to their involvement with high-needs youth and continue to do the work because they feel that they are an integral part of a team that creates positive change in young people and their overall community. Foster parents feel a sense of belonging and support from our other foster parents and the program. Foster parents are ambassadors for OCP and help recruit prospective foster parents through sharing positive stories.

- ◆ **Treatment foster parents view their interventions and efforts with youth as planting seeds for long-term change and positive futures.** Foster parents can answer the question, "What's my reason for being a treatment foster parent?" The investment that foster parents apply to youth now impacts family values, communication practices, positive relationship strategies, work ethic, parenting practices, and many other considerations that play a part in the success of multiple generations ahead. Foster parents are a resource for multiple youth over time, not just one, and through their efforts youth exit systems of care to permanency.

---

2 Chamberlain, P., & Reid, J. (1998). Comparison of two community alternatives to incarceration for chronic juvenile offenders. *Journal of Consulting and Clinical Psychology*, 6, 624-633.

Chamberlain, P. (2003). The Oregon Multidimensional Treatment Foster Care model: Features, outcomes, and progress in dissemination. In S. Schoenwald & S. Henggeler (Series Eds.), Moving evidence-based treatments from the laboratory into clinical practice. *Cognitive and Behavioral Practice*, 10, 303-312.

Evaluation Methodology

The aim of our evaluation was to see what kind and quality of impact Oregon Community Programs is having on the treatment foster parents within in our Treatment Foster Care Oregon (TFCO) program. To understand this, we explored two broad evaluation questions:

1. What kind and quality of impact are we having on our treatment foster parents?
2. What aspects of our program are causing this impact?

Over the course of the project, we (a) developed and refined our ideas of intended impact and indicators, (b) designed and implemented a mixed methods outcome evaluation using both qualitative and quantitative means to collect and analyze data, (c) identified themes and findings, and (d) considered the implications to those findings for program improvement and innovation.

This project began by identifying and clarifying the intended impact of Oregon Community Programs. Once the ideas of impact had been developed, we used the Heart Triangle™ model to identify qualitative and quantitative indicators of impact on the mental, behavioral, and emotional changes in our treatment foster parents. We used these indicators to design a qualitative interview protocol and a quantitative questionnaire to evaluate progress toward achieving our intended impact.

Qualitative Data Collection and Analysis

For the qualitative portion of the evaluation, we designed an in-depth interview protocol to gain data about the structural, qualitative changes resulting from our program. We delimited our population to all current treatment foster parents and a handful of former foster parents. Our population size for this evaluation was 25. We used a purposeful stratified sampling technique to select a representative sample from the population we serve. Our sample size was 17, drawn from the following strata of our population:

- Fostering status (current vs former foster parents)
- Number of placements (two or less vs more than two)

- ◆ Number of caregivers (single vs two-parent homes)
- ◆ Other children in the home (families with vs families without biological children at home)

Our interview team consisted of Executive Director Ana Day, Program Director Kym Broten, Clinical Project Manager, Nicolle Kuhn, Program Manager Jaimie Broadhead, and Billing/Outcomes Specialist Alice Wheeler. We convened one-on-one interviews lasting from between 45 minutes and one hour in length and collected interview data using handwritten notes and/or the Otter voice-to-text transcription app. Treatment foster parents were compensated for providing their perspectives with a $100 VISA gift card.

We then analyzed the data inductively using a modified version of thematic analysis. Each interviewer analyzed the data from their interviews individually to identify initial themes. Together, we developed common themes from all of the interviews collectively. We identified the overarching and inter-interview themes that emerged from the full scope of our data analysis to illuminate the collective insights and discoveries. We grouped the feedback into categories and examined the dynamics among the themes and relationships between the themes that were revealed in the data. We then determined the most significant and meaningful discoveries and brought them forward as findings.

Quantitative Data Collection and Analysis

For the quantitative portion of the evaluation, we designed a questionnaire to collect data on our quantitative indicators of impact. We administered this instrument to 17 treatment foster parents and had a response of 14, a response rate of 82%. The data were analyzed primarily using measures of central tendency. We identified key insights, patterns, and gaps within the data and incorporated these discoveries into the related findings. The most significant insights from the quantitative data are described in the following narrative.

Limitations

Many of our treatment foster parents are co-parenting couples, but typically only one member of the pair was interviewed. The sample size for foster parents was relatively small. Although we were able to invite input from all current treatment foster parents, staff time constraints allowed only limited sampling of former foster parents.

Findings

Finding 1: Professional foster parents are grown, not found.

Key Insight: Foster parents do not begin as professionals but become professionals over time as they develop their skills and grow from their experiences.

A common focus when recruiting treatment foster parents is the need to find "diamonds," caregivers who come preloaded with the knowledge, skills, and abilities to parent complex youth. Such a focus leads programs to emphasize recruitment marketing for an overly narrow target population. Our data suggest that with the type of supports and training offered by TFCO, a much larger cohort of caregivers can achieve paraprofessional status, expanding an otherwise limited community resource. In other words, TFCO doesn't just look for diamonds; some of our diamonds are "in the rough" at recruitment and start to shine with time, experience, and on-the-job training.

Our data demonstrate that foster parents improve their skills as they experience and navigate challenges with the support of the program. Experienced foster parents consistently noted that learning to use the TFCO program, although not always intuitive at first, resulted in improved connection with youth, feeling effective in helping youth accomplish their goals, and in increased confidence that they could provide treatment to youth with complex behavioral health presentations. In this way, they become increasingly skilled and valuable as treatment resources with each successful placement in a process of continuous quality improvement that benefits the community.

A 15-year veteran foster parent offered her perspective on gaining experience and capability over time, saying,

[When I got stuck] I think being able to process even after the fact with someone at OCP was really helpful. The same [situations] come up again, so I would feel better prepared. More and more confident that what I had done was the right approach or if I needed to make an adjustment. Being able to talk that over in a supported setting was really helpful...to see if there were any alternatives for how to respond.

In our survey sample, the majority of respondents reported significant growth in the following key skills development areas:

- Identify an alternative prosocial behavior to problem behaviors you've noticed
- Keep aware of youth whereabouts and activities
- Collaborate with the Team Lead before starting a new intervention
- Tell youth about expectations or plans ahead of time (pre-teaching)
- Monitor homework and school behavior
- Pay a lot more attention to when kids are doing the right thing
- Connect with youth as a supportive and nurturing mentor
- Notice when you have gotten caught in a power struggle without judging yourself
- Manage your own stress
- Help youth navigate important family relationships, even when complicated or imperfect.

As a result of growing confidence in their skills and abilities, most foster parents also reported increased confidence in their ability to serve challenging youth and to be an ongoing foster parent for future youth in need (see Figures 1 and 2).

Significance

In their training process, treatment foster parents must unlearn and then learn new strategies to manage youth behavior, develop their own competencies, and monitor stress. In many professions, there is

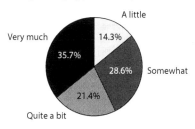

Figure 1. Since being a part of OCP, I have grown more comfortable taking challenging youth into my home. (n=14)

Percentage of participant responses

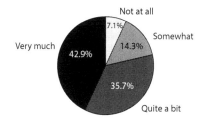

Figure 2. Since being a part of OCP, my confidence in taking multiple youth placements over time has increased. (n=14)

Percentage of participant responses

an understanding that early investment in the workforce cultivates an important future resource. Treatment foster parents are a special kind of workforce—a volunteer workforce. At any point, they can end their participation, and the community loses a critical resource for youth.

In the State of Oregon, the number of youth needing treatment foster care far exceeds the number of qualified providers. Strategies that focus on identifying foster parents who are already supremely skilled miss opportunities to expand the volunteer workforce sufficiently to meet the need. Additionally, these strategies often fail to expand the diversity and representation of potential foster parents who could be trained to provide outstanding care with the right type of guidance and oversight.

Possible Responses

Adjustments

- ◆ Provide additional or different training in the areas where survey respondents reported needing more training, especially helping the youth navigate important family relationships, even when complicated or imperfect (71% of foster parents reported that more training in this area would be helpful.)

- Provide education and advocacy to foster care certification and licensing bodies to emphasize that the "on the job training" of TFCO is a valuable strategy to increase local and statewide capacity.
- Better articulate the necessary foundational qualities of families that can be cultivated into a good fit for TFCO
- Consideration and caution around potential equity discrepancies.

New Strategies

- By casting a wider recruitment net, the logical conclusion is that more good fit AND poor fit homes may start the certification process. The program might benefit by exploring and refining the stages of onboarding prospective families and what indicators exist that a family is on or off track with skills development, along with potential remedies (see "mindset shift").
- Advocating for rule changes to increase diverse and representative treatment foster families by ending rules that require 50% of direct care staff to have a bachelor's degree and/or provide an alternative option that emphasizes lived experience and cultural representation.

Experiments

- Establish and mark levels of skill development for new families at intervals and explore what factors move families more/less quickly along the path.

Finding 2: Foster parents' motivation comes from within.

Key Insight: Successful foster parents are most motivated by seeing the growth they help bring about in youth through their interventions and efforts.

Although stereotypes of foster parents who collect checks from the state persist, our data show that the reality is foster parents' commitment is primarily driven by internal motivation rather than financial compensation. This evaluation showed that the factors most motivating for foster parents are: (1) witnessing the youth in their home learn and demonstrate positive skills and abilities over the time they are in treatment foster homes and (2) observing foster children who too often are burdened with adult worries start to play and behave with childlike lightheartedness.

Nearly every foster parent interviewed commented that they feel especially energized when they see the youth in their home accomplish something that they couldn't do before.

We noted that the accomplishments were often modest in scope—moving from shyness to participation in sports, learning to make dinner, getting caught up on homework—but were experienced as highly encouraging for foster parents. Eighty-six percent of foster parents surveyed noted a significant increase in their ability to see the long-term positive difference they are making (see Figure 3).

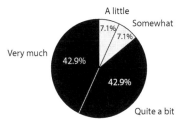

Figure 3. Since being a part of OCP, I am better able to see the long-term positive difference I am making on the youth in my home. (n=14)

Percentage of participant responses

A newer foster parent reflected on the growth of a youth in her home:

He [was] just so sad all the time. You know, like almost depressed all the time. He would never talk and didn't ever want to do anything fun, and was always so quiet. I always was like, man, he hates us! He hates being here! It just felt like that because he was so reserved, I guess. And [then] to see him being so successful and doing things that he would never do before, like getting a job and saving money and being outgoing at church. Going and doing things that he would not normally do on his own. He talked to us every day and shared with us what's happening in his life. It's just amazing to see this kid who had their shell completely closed to now having an open shell. Being willing to talk and willing to participate, and willing to show that he cares. He shared feelings and emotions. It's just so amazing to see them from where they start to where they end. There's no better feeling than knowing that I've been able to be there to support them and get them to where they are now.

Several parents also noted that it is sometimes hard to remember or access accomplishments, especially when there are challenging behaviors competing for attention. In these times, it was helpful when the program reminded them of growth. For example, noticing that problem behaviors on Parent Daily Reports were decreasing.

One long-term foster parent shared, "I like to keep a list of accomplishments…things that are positive. And then you look at those things, and it really helps me personally."

Additionally, multiple interviews highlighted that treatment foster parents consistently notice that the youth in their home exhibit behaviors that are atypical for youth of their age experiencing normative development. Many youth referred for treatment show "parentified" behavior. In other words, they have developed behaviors that are normally reserved for parents (e.g., worrying about money, taking care of younger siblings, too much adult information) at an unusually young age. As described by an interviewee,

So many of these kids don't have those boundaries or expectations appropriately set up. It puts so much burden on them to make [adult] choices. For young children, that's not age-appropriate, right? I mean, that's something they would start doing in 10 years, not when they're three, four, and five and on up....It's a relief for them to bump up against that boundary, to feel somebody hold the line for them...It takes away a burden.

Foster parents interviewed report that many of the youth entering the program have missed childhood experiences or demonstrate adult worries or stresses. When kids acclimate to the program, foster parents notice that the youth start to laugh or play more wholeheartedly, like their peers. Observing this shift is one of the commonly reported areas that generate fulfillment and satisfaction for foster parents and often leads to hope that youth can achieve other important goals like higher education and employment. Other foster parents commented that they see the work as "breaking dysfunctional family patterns" and "giving kids a mental picture of what a functional family can look like."

Significance

Recruitment and retention strategies often focus on extrinsic motivators for foster parents. While it is certainly necessary to reimburse treatment foster parents in a way that honors their skills and commitment of time and energy for youth in need, it is important to highlight that in the long run, treatment foster parents are motivated by the fulfillment of seeing youth change.

It is also important to understand that the types of youth growth that provide fulfillment and joy for foster parents are often small steps or humble beginnings. It is seeing the forward movement in youth more than the actual accomplishment itself that compels foster parents to continue.

Possible Responses

Adjustments

- Team Leads can highlight when foster parents share even small stories about youth developing new skills or increasingly behaving in an age-appropriate way.
- Team Leads can help establish the causal connection between the foster parent treatment efforts and these results to energize and encourage foster parents.

New Strategies

Shining a light on specific stories or examples of skill mastery or youth relaxing into age-appropriate play in recruitment materials may improve engagement or interest for potential foster parents by highlighting common motivation. Using photos or graphics that convey similar themes may also be helpful.

Finding 3: Feeling connected to a team is the key to retention.

Key Insight: Foster parent peer support accelerates learning and buffers secondary trauma and toxic stress. Program support takes unnecessary burdens off foster parents and improves their ability to respond to youths' treatment needs.

Foster parents often begin fostering with idealistic thoughts about what the experience will be like. Experiencing the reality of the day-to-day struggles of foster parenting can be discouraging at first. Our inquiry found that more than two-thirds of the foster parents interviewed reported that their views about the role of a foster parent changed very much or quite a bit as a result of their experience with the OCP training program.

Additionally, most foster parents interviewed described that working on a team was hugely important for keeping them motivated and engaged. Specifically, hearing the experiences of other foster parents in the weekly foster parent meeting was experienced as normalizing difficulties and building hope that progress can be made. Survey results indicated that as they participated in the OCP program, foster parents became more comfortable being vulnerable with one another and trusting the support and advice from other foster parents (see Figures 4 and 5).

Qualitative interviews included multiple examples of the importance of program and peer support. As one foster parent put it,

It can feel like, man, I gotta be the only person going through this! So, a lot of times, just hearing the similar struggles from other parents and maybe different ways that they've dealt with it helps. Sometimes I'll hear [other FPs] say something. I'll be like, 'Hey, I'm gonna have to try

Figure 4. Since being a part of OCP, I am more comfortable being vulnerable in the foster parent group. (n=14)

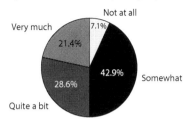

Percentage of participant responses

Figure 5. Since being a part of OCP, I have grown in my ability to trust support and advice from other foster parents. (n=14)

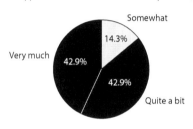

Percentage of participant responses

that next time!' So just, basically, the 'you're not alone' kind of feeling when you hear people going through similar challenges.

Another foster parent shared about the foster parent group,

It normalizes it to a certain extent. You can approach it maybe in a different way or give an idea [to someone else] how to approach it in a different way. There was always good feedback about stuff or so often to just have a good laugh! It does lighten it because it feels really heavy sometimes. Especially when you first read the case history, you know. It can be very disturbing. I think it is good to relieve some of that tension there and share those feelings.

In summary, the peer support and team approach of TFCO was reported as very helpful in stabilizing and encouraging foster parents and motivating them to continue. One experienced foster parent noted that it helps to hear from someone who had lived through it before and offered the following advice to newer foster parents,

> *Just give yourself a break when you maybe don't handle things the way you wanted to. Use it to learn from rather than to beat yourself up. I tended to give myself a hard time when I saw where I could have done things better, but you know, we all go through challenges.*

Significance

Very few treatment foster parent programs offer the level of peer support that is offered by TFCO, and it is perhaps one of the most critical components of the program. The team approach also shelters foster parents from non-treatment-related system demands, which improves longevity and capacity to focus on youth needs. The complexity of foster youths' decision-making teams has increased in recent years, and even with program support, it has significantly increased non-treatment-related demands on foster parents. Scheduling alone can be a time-consuming task when a youth has multiple adults on their case (caseworker, CASA, attorney, ICWA worker, permanency worker, wraparound coordinator, ILP liaison, etc.).

Within the TFCO model, the foster parent is prioritized as the primary treatment provider for the youth. The Team Lead shoulders many of the case management and scheduling demands to free up the foster parent to be quickly responsive to youth needs and to implement the treatment plan in the foster home. TFCO is unique in this respect—most other treatment foster care settings task the foster parent with managing logistics like scheduling home visits, respite, updating multiple system partners, etc. Foster parents find it very supportive to rely on the program to navigate scheduling and communication with multiple stakeholders, improving efficiency and reducing miscommunication.

Possible Responses

Adjustments

◆ Refine the process for introducing the youth's decision-making team to the TFCO communication process and the value of starting inquiries with the Team Lead, especially when the youth's state worker is unfamiliar with the TFCO model or the team is very large.

New Strategies

◆ Continue to adapt to the changes/challenges associated with balancing in-person support and video conferencing options, including investing in technology that makes hybrid meetings feel more natural.

◆ Advocate to reduce unnecessary administrative burdens on treatment foster parents.

Experiments

◆ Shift to a hybrid foster parent meeting model permanently in which most meetings are virtual, but there is an option for in person participation in all meetings. Maintaining some frequency of in-person meetings would still be a priority.

Finding 4: A "mindset shift" that makes fostering more fulfilling.

Key Insight: Foster parents who learn to use the key TFCO skills experience a shift that makes the work easier, more enjoyable, and more effective.

Our data show that many foster parents were surprised that TFCO asks them both to learn and unlearn parenting skills. Often, they found that the strategies and skills that they utilized in parenting their own children needed to be supplemented or even let go as their skill in implementing TFCO expanded. To illustrate, 86% of surveyed foster parents reported that their confidence in using TFCO strategies had increased "very much" or "quite a bit." Fourteen percent of respondents said their confidence had grown "somewhat" or "not at all." Although challenging at first, this unlearning often yielded significant benefits. One foster parent interviewed describes how she experienced a key learning moment:

For me, unlearning would be the controlling piece of it. It actually has taught me to be a better mom all around, honestly, which is kind of funny. Because I have always been so controlling of my own children, and then I'm realizing the more controlling you are, and the more you push their buttons and try and tighten them in, the more they're going to want to do the opposite.

Another foster parent offered:

I had my doubts at first that this method was going to work. We're old school, you know. Things were done a little bit differently with my children as a whole. But I wanted to learn new techniques, and I am glad that I have been a part of this.

As foster parents develop skills and experience, they tend to endorse program skills more emphatically; for instance, the importance of skills like high supervision and monitoring of youth and paying more attention to what kids are doing well than what needs to be corrected. Families who grasp these concepts become motivated to think creatively to increase success. The following foster parent describes the TFCO model's approach to adjusting caregiver strategies to improve youth outcomes,

So, in my mind, I was always having to think, well, how could I tweak this to do a better job at managing this child's behavior? Who could I talk to about that? What resource could I look at to kind of redefine to have my responses provoke the response I wanted to see from the child? So, it's just continually finding new ways, alternative ways to deal with behaviors or attitudes that the child would have had.

A common refrain in our data was that treatment foster parents typically did not appreciate the value of "role stratification" initially, but once they experienced the value, it resulted in meaningful improvement for both them and the youth. Role stratification in TFCO is the effort to create a team of support staff who target specific needs and skills for the youth so that treatment foster parent has support. Chief among role stratification strategies is the assignment of "limit setter" to the Team Lead in order to allow the treatment foster parent more flexibility to align with the youth to navigate challenges. For instance, the Team Lead might privately consult with the treatment foster parent about the dress code limits for the upcoming school dance. They would develop some parameters for what is permitted and prohibited, and the Team Lead would deliver that message to the youth. If the news was disappointing to the youth, then that negative energy is directed to the Team Lead rather than the foster parent. This allows an increased degree of freedom for the treatment parent to align with and support the youth with navigating requirements and diminishes power struggles.

One foster parent offers the following about how she came to recognize the value of letting the program be the limit setter for the youth,

The moment that I started doing that, it became so much easier. Every kid after that kid, it was like, okay, I think I understand the model. That's why it's so important to do it that way now. It is probably the biggest thing that I've learned: to be a support for the kid and to let the program do all the rest of it. And that's just made my life and, honestly, the kid's life, either way, easier than when it was a back and forth between me and them.

She went on to describe that the value of role stratification is primarily for the youth, who may be expecting conflict in caregiving situations:

It's so nice to be able to only be the support person and to keep that good relationship with the kid no matter what is happening. Because then [the kids] don't feel disconnected from us in the home. They can disconnect from the people that are giving them the consequences [Team Lead] but feel fully supported and loved here.

Interestingly, when surveyed about how much more likely they are to utilize role stratification since participating with OCP, there was a notable split in responses. Fifty-seven percent of those surveyed said they were "very likely" to use role stratification, and 43% reported they were "somewhat" more likely (see Figure 6).

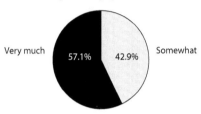

Figure 6. Since being a part of OCP, I am more likely to use role stratification (letting your Team Lead be the limit-setter) to manage challenging behaviors. (n=14)

Percentage of participant responses

We hypothesize that this split might reflect the different stages of growth for treatment foster parents. It might be enlightening to further explore whether treatment foster parents who are less likely to use role stratification (or other key program components) exit foster caring sooner than foster parents who endorse seeing the value in those strategies.

Significance

If a mindset shift indicates that a treatment foster parent is poised to become more successful and fulfilled, then adjusting approaches to achieve that shift (or achieve it more quickly) becomes important both for treatment efficacy and longevity of treatment parents.

Possible Responses

Adjustments

- Assess whether FPs have demonstrated such a shift and identify what factors most contribute in order to accelerate it.
- Consider if the youth placed with foster parents who don't clearly make the mindset shift have different treatment success rates.

New Strategies

- Get further feedback from FPs about what contributes to this mindset shift. When did they experience it? What made the difference? Is there a way they could've arrived there more quickly or with less suffering?
- Overtly discuss these findings with our treatment foster parent group and share a summary of the findings for further input.

Experiments

- Experiment with randomly assigning new foster parents to shorter vs longer shaping curve (i.e., try to initiate mindset shift more quickly)
- Monitor for how race, ethnicity, language, or other cultural factors may intersect with this work.

Finding 5: Different family structures have different support needs.

Key Insight: Single parents and parents with their own minor children in the home face unique challenges as foster parents that must be taken into account in designing effective supports.

Although all foster parents sometimes need a break, our data show that single foster parents have fewer natural options for self-care than co-parenting foster parents. With two caregivers in the home, each parent can "tag out" when needed to re-regulate, recharge, or otherwise manage stress. Single households tend to rely more on the Team Lead to buffer their relationship with the youth when limits need to be set, for example when the Team Lead intervenes to set limits in a manner that allows the caregiver to remain aligned with the foster youth. This role stratification reduces power struggles and caregiver stress substantially across caregiver types but is of particular value for single parents.

Additionally, the financial cost of supervision for youth is higher for single-parenting foster parents. Within the TFCO model, program youth are required to be supervised by an adult at all times. In co-parenting households, supervision is more easily changed over, but in single-parent homes, foster parents must often identify other supervision resources that can meet the needs of their youth, which typically are of substantial cost.

Similarly, our data show that foster parents (both single and dual) with their own minor children in the home have specific worries related to perceived risk and safety for those children. Parents express concern with buffering their children from modeling of problem behavior or worrying about the risk of physical harm. In our data, foster parents with their own children in the home typically noted that if something dangerous occurred, that would decrease their ability to continue fostering. Typically, program support was identified as helping reduce these risks. One foster mother with young children described the biggest factor for her in considering whether she can continue fostering, saying,

> For me, it has been probably the treatment of my kids. I have kids that have totally loved my children. And then I've had kids that have totally been bothered by my children and have even used them as an excuse for why they weren't successful. Probably the biggest worry when I have a kid, is how they're going to treat my kids because it's been different with every kiddo. And even though I do think it's really good for my children to understand different people's backgrounds and where they're coming from, it's still hard for them to figure out because they're pretty little.

Significance

It is worth mentioning that TFCO foster parents of many family constellations can be successful in implementing the program and helping youth achieve their treatment goals. Some youth referred do better in a single-parent home, and matching youth needs with foster home strengths is a core tenet of the program. We believe with the right supports, even youth with significant behavioral challenges can benefit from TFCO in a single-parent household, so identifying supports that keep it manageable are critical.

By providing supports targeted to the specific needs of different family compositions, foster families will provide better support to program youth and experience more satisfaction from their work.

Possible Responses
Adjustments

- Orient new foster families who are single parenting or parenting with children to the importance of self-care, supervision, and role stratification. Provide more targeted follow-up.
- Expand the set of approved "helpers" for each family.
- Advocate for common sense regulatory changes that could expand access to helpers while still maintaining youth safety, such as:
    - Extending the length of time approved helpers are allowed to provide care (some programs limit to only 3 hours at a time).
    - Increase the allowable number of approved helpers for single parents, which are currently limited by the criminal background check unit, to a maximum of four.

New Strategies

- Consider easing the financial burden on single parents to access quality supervision resources by:
    - Identifying program-approved respite options and supporting the use of "by the hour" childcare.
    - Investigate partnerships with a few high-quality childcare options to ease access.

Experiments

- Increase reimbursement stipends for enriching childcare for single parents. Some challenges might be how to do this in an equitable way.

Conclusion

Insights Into Impact

When we initiated this program evaluation project, we hoped to better understand how our treatment foster parent recruitment and training program was functioning, especially with regard to how effective we are in motivating foster caregivers to continue their work for multiple youth. We hoped that participation was fulfilling for treatment foster parents and would encourage ongoing participation.

After examining the results of our qualitative and quantitative research, we have a better understanding of some of the specific areas where we are often successful and where we might target our energies to improve. We are proud that our efforts to cultivate foster parent peer support were highlighted by so many as a critical component of their learning and motivation for perseverance. It was gratifying to see how the Team Lead contact was experienced by treatment parents as both supportive and a source of growth.

Steps Forward

As first steps in utilizing these findings to improve our programming, we are planning to target the following primary objectives:

1. Speak to underlying motivations in marketing. We plan to target marketing efforts to highlight the factors that we have learned are most meaningful and fulfilling to foster parents. For example, we might feature images or stories about youth mastering new skills or learning how to let go of adult worries to engage the attention of prospective foster parents.

2. Make virtual meetings safe for vulnerability and learning. While we had originally imagined a full return to in-person meetings, our foster parents have shown that hybrid meetings have some benefit to them if we can use technology well. We are looking into different platforms for this purpose so that the peer support can continue. Helping keep a safe and natural feeling is important to encourage vulnerability and support.

3. Advocate with funders and regulatory bodies. We believe that sharing some of these findings and perspectives may be compelling to state and community decision makers to illustrate some of the areas where regulation might be adjusted to support the goals of expanding the capacity of safe, high-quality, evidence-based treatment foster care. We hope that the data from this project can help illustrate the opportunity to invest in programs that add capacity to the treatment foster care system.

Opportunities for Future Evaluation

Our team was most energized to further explore the concept of a "mindset shift" that treatment foster parents experience and the implications for the quality of treatment and retention of foster parents. Further study might yield adjustments and new strategies that could help us achieve mastery of program components more quickly or with less stress.

Our team also discussed how we might investigate strategies to mark advancing competency in the TFCO model more overtly for treatment foster parents. We observed that the treatment foster parents in our program are at varying places in their development of key skills and that better pinpointing where in their growth trajectory they are might be helpful in providing targeting support or training to advance them to the "mindset shift" point where long-term retention is more likely and sustainable. TFCO emphasizes shaping and learning on the job as an effective and engaging tool for pacing learning, but there might be some specific intervention points where more targeted feedback might create change more quickly.

Finally, while this project focused on the impact OCP has within our foster parent training program, the ultimate OCP mission is to provide effective treatment to our youth participants and their families. To that end, our foster care programs plan to prioritize developing qualitative interview questions to be targeted at the youth graduates that can be delivered near youth graduation dates. If possible, we would love to explore offering the opportunity to provide feedback to both recent and past graduates of our programs. As part of this process, we created some preliminary outlines of intended impacts and indicators on youth participants. Developing these into an interview that can be delivered near youth graduation dates and, ideally, at some interval post-graduation would likely yield important information about longer-term impacts.

Be Your Best Cottage Grove

Finding our Place

Jody Rolnick, Samantha Duncan, Vanessa Vogel, Ayesha Talreja

Organization and Program Overview

Be Your Best Cottage Grove formed in 2013 in response to the release of the first countywide Community Health Needs Assessment, which showed a disproportionate number of South Lane residents in poor health with corresponding high morbidity and mortality. Alarmed by the data, dozens of individuals, social service providers, faith-based organizations, businesses, government representatives, and funders rallied for an innovative approach to our community's health crisis. The wide array of stakeholders unified around the mission and vision: To create, through collective action, a brighter future for our rural community by ensuring access to the services and supports people need to be their best.

Be Your Best Cottage Grove is dedicated to improving community vitality in South Lane County by:

- Fostering a network of community builders to successfully lead, and participate in, collaborative projects;
- Stewarding the collaborative process and learnings; and
- Modeling the work.

More than 80 community-based and regional partners comprise Be Your Best, which meets monthly to identify community needs and opportunities and together create strategies to leverage expertise and resources to address community problems. The collective impact systems-change model serves as our collaborative's operational guide, and core values include a commitment to open and honest dialogue, an emphasis on equity, and cultivating and sharing continuous learning.

Be Your Best relies on community-based volunteer leadership, advocacy, and grassroots momentum to carry projects to success. Be Your Best has served as a rural Community Health Improvement Plan workgroup for Live Healthy Lane. Also, participating partners have collaborated on assorted local projects addressing health disparities and social determinants of health, including activating a crisis response network for COVID pandemic response, establishing immunization clinics for children from undocumented families, and implementing a multifaceted, multi-year maternal wellness program.

Much of our work has been done in alignment with the goals and priorities of both the Lane County and the PeaceHealth Cottage Grove Community Medical Center Community Health Needs Assessments (CHA) and Community Health Improvement Plans (CHP).

Be Your Best recently became a registered Oregon nonprofit corporation and is seeking federal 501c3 tax-exempt status. At this time, United Way of Lane County is Be Your Best's fiscal sponsor and applicant for (and holder of) grant funds.

Intended Impact

At the beginning of the study, Be Your Best's intended impacts were to:

◆ **Harness the energy of many and varied voices to effect broad-scale change and increase equitable opportunities for all South Lane County community members, especially the most vulnerable and disenfranchised.** People who participate in Be Your Best (whether as a volunteer or an employee of an organization) are committed to a network of strategic thinkers and doers working in tandem to problem-solve and change systems and conditions so everyone in the community can get what they need to be their very best selves. Partners value coalition building from the ground up and gathering input from people who are most profoundly impacted. Partners also prize and practice clear communication, mutual respect, and creative problem-solving.

◆ **Work together to bridge gaps in the system and build capacity for priority projects/targets.** People who participate in Be Your Best see how working together towards a shared goal (in projects large and small) attracts external funding and interest. BYB partners understand deeply how to identify gaps in services and resource allocation and find ways to wrap around providers and build more capacity. BYB members value stretching themselves beyond their comfort zone and knowledge base and derive gratification from learning new skills, making deep social connections, and being involved in helping their community become a better place for all.

◆ **Develop measurements for evaluating and understanding progress toward shared goals.** People who participate in Be Your Best learn the importance of program/project evaluation and how to create and track progress so that everyone can see when efforts are making real (vs. imagined) headway and whether or not their work/projects/programs are actually improving lives.

Evaluation Methodology

The aim of our evaluation was to see what kind and quality of impact Be Your Best Cottage Grove is having on its partners. To understand this, we explored two broad evaluation questions:

◆ What kind and quality of impact are we having on people who participate in the network?

◆ What aspects of our program are causing this impact?

Over the course of the project, we (a) developed and refined our ideas of intended impact and indicators, (b) designed and implemented a mixed methods outcome evaluation using both qualitative and quantitative means to collect and analyze data, (c) identified themes and findings, and (d) considered the implications to those findings for program improvement and innovation.

This project began by identifying and clarifying the intended impact of Be Your Best. Once the ideas of impact had been developed, we used the *Heart Triangle*™ model to identify qualitative and quantitative indicators of impact on the mental, behavioral, and emotional changes in network participants. We used these indicators to design a qualitative interview protocol and a quantitative questionnaire to evaluate progress toward achieving our intended impact.

Qualitative Data Collection and Analysis

For the qualitative portion of the evaluation, we designed an in-depth interview protocol to gain data about the structural, qualitative changes resulting from our program. Our population size for this evaluation was about 200. We used a purposeful stratified sampling technique to select a representative sample of about 20, drawn from the following strata of our population:

- Region: Metro, rural, South Lane County, North Douglas County
- Service Sector: Government, Social Services, Private Business/ Entrepreneur, Healthcare, School District, Grassroots, Faith-based
- Role in Organization: Executive, Supervisory, Frontline Employee, Volunteer/Board Member

Our interview team consisted of Jody, Samantha, Vanessa, and Ayesha. We convened one-on-one interviews lasting from between 45 minutes and one hour in length and collected interview data using handwritten notes.

We then analyzed the data inductively using a modified version of thematic analysis. Each interviewer analyzed the data from their interviews individually to identify initial themes. Together, we developed common themes from all of the interviews collectively. We identified the overarching and inter-interview themes that emerged from the full scope of our data analysis to illuminate the collective insights and discoveries. We mapped these themes visually and examined the dynamics among the themes, causes and catalysts of the themes, new or surprising insights related to the themes, and relationships between the themes that were revealed in the data. We then determined the most significant and meaningful discoveries and brought them forward as findings.

Quantitative Data Collection and Analysis

For the quantitative portion of the evaluation, we designed a questionnaire to collect data on our quantitative indicators of impact. We administered this instrument to the 220 people on our 2020 listserv and had a response of 22, a 10% response rate. The data were analyzed primarily using measures of central tendency. We identified key insights, patterns, and gaps within the data and incorporated these discoveries into the related findings. The most significant insights from the quantitative data are described in the following narrative.

Limitations

The evaluation was conducted during the COVID-19 pandemic. During the data collection stage, the country was in the midst of the COVID-19 pandemic. This may have resulted in several limitations, including smaller qualitative and quantitative sample sizes than originally intended.

Findings

Finding 1: A safe place

Key Insight: Be Your Best has laid the foundation for creating opportunities for inclusivity and meaningful conversation around complex and difficult topics without judgment, fear of retribution, or exclusion.

Many of those interviewed said they found Be Your Best to be a safe and grounding space where they could practice speaking up, asking hard questions, challenging assumptions, reflecting, and learning — skills that helped them be better community builders and establish trust among and between partners.

"Be Your Best gives me strength," said one person, voicing a common theme that emerged from our survey: Individuals involved in Be Your Best say they feel empowered, on a grassroots level, to make a difference knowing they have the network behind them. "Personal relationships I have built [through BYB] have added to my connections," said one person. "Being part of BYB has been enlightening, informative and uplifting to me," said another.

At the same time, those interviewed expressed disappointment that there aren't more executive-level leaders also making an active effort to grow and sustain the collective community voice. As one person explained: "I am trying to get others in leadership to understand the value of front-end investment in resolving an issue versus waiting until the problem is too big to ignore."

Responses to the survey — while validating that Be Your Best creates opportunities for personal and professional growth — also reveal additional opportunities for improvement. For example, when asked how being involved with the network has impacted how they show up in the community, 63% of people said 'very much' or 'quite a bit', with less than 23% responding 'somewhat' or 'a little (See Figure 1).'

Figure 1. How has your involvement with Be Your Best impacted your role in the community? - I am showing up differently. (n=22)

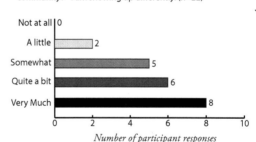

Number of participant responses

Several people said they welcome more opportunities for exploration, self-reflection, sharing, and celebrating.

Significance

This finding validates Be Your Best's original emphasis on the value and impacts of collective action by like-minded individuals who center the community. Recruitment of more executive leaders will build a stronger and more effective network.

Possible Responses

Adjustments

- Amend the format of meetings to include time and space for deep reflection and sharing.
- Tap ambassadors to recruit executive- and state- and county-level individuals to engage with the broader BYB network on a regular basis.

New Strategies

- Identify and deploy appropriate advocates to ask hard questions and lift up issues/barriers.

Experiments

- With intention, meet to process check, debrief, and share results.

Finding 2: What do you do?

Key Insight: It is unclear how Be Your Best operates and what its primary work is, opening the door for the organization and work to be misunderstood, misinterpreted, and/or misrepresented.

In interviews, several people expressed continued confusion about the purpose of Be Your Best. While they see Be Your Best as the connector to the community and to a network of others who are doing a lot of good work, they don't distinguish it from other monthly meeting commitments that feature many of the same people and cover the same topics. One executive-level leader said,

At first, because it wasn't clear what the purpose was, I was 'against' Be Your Best. People were trying to collaborate but weren't trained for it or

had experience in it. As a result, I felt ganged up on and all interactions felt very adversarial.

Over time, the interviewee said, connections were clarified and trust restored to the point that "now I really value the relationships — and understand the intentions."

People surveyed said they think Be Your Best is in competition for scarce resources, is seen as a gatekeeper for connections with high-level funding, government entities, and rural populations, and is run by 'others' with a pre-set agenda rather than the collective pursuing a shared goal. Even long-time participants do not necessarily identify themselves as Be Your Best and point to others (mainly the administrative coordinator) as doing a great job.

Those interviewed also said they worry that projects "chosen," "endorsed," or prioritized for support by BYB may be due to favoritism. Interviewees were also unclear about what Be Your Best "support" of a project or initiative looks like or how things move forward. "People want someone to take the lead and without a champion, projects can easily fizzle out, which is frustrating," said another person interviewed.

This finding may contribute to survey results which show possible hesitancy (and room for improvement) in engaging people in the network. According to the survey results, just 45% of people involved with Be Your Best said they have 'very much' developed a habit of advocating for collaborative efforts to increase impact, while 54% categorize their habit as 'somewhat' or 'quite a bit (see Figure 2).'

Figure 2. Through my participation in Be Your Best, I have developed a habit of advocating for collaborative efforts to increase impact. (n=22)

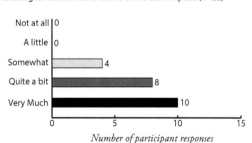

Number of participant responses

Still, many people seem to grasp what the network is about. "Be Your Best has been a tireless advocate for the vulnerable in Cottage Grove communities and is doing a great job," said one survey respondent. "I think Be Your Best is a very unique, positive, informative and supportive collaboration of community members," said another.

Significance

This finding is noteworthy but not surprising: During COVID, some of the ongoing informal operational (and perception) challenges that were easier to overlook when people felt really connected during in-person Be Your Best meetings are now more glaringly obvious. With the online meeting format, it feels harder to be truly engaged and more easily excluded — which is contrary to Be Your Best's intentions. Be Your Best aspires to model inclusivity and foster opportunities that result in a richer experience and more informed solutions for a more systemic and sustainable impact for our community.

Possible Responses

Adjustments

- Hold a series of listening sessions to help identify and operationalize key values.
- Collaboratively create an operational framework.

New Strategies

- Offer more training and skill-building opportunities/focus to build value in attendance/participation.
- Work on defining roles/responsibilities for how to have effective collective/collaborative action.

Experiments

- Create space on BYB website or other widely accessible electronic platform for archives of everything from skill-building trainings to links to resources to initiatives (history, actions taken, meeting minutes, etc.).

Finding 3: Collaboration = Chaos

Key Insight: Working in collaboration can be frustrating. It's hard to see progress, to know when and how to take action, and to know whose responsibility it is for keeping others on task.

While people said they like being part of a network that is doing good in the community, many interviewed did not identify themselves as Be Your Best, instead pointing to others to keep things moving forward. "Shared leadership and consensus models, by their very nature, can be challenging," said one interviewee. "Sometimes with BYB, I wonder who's in charge, and are we really having action?"

An abundance of patience and persistence are required when working in tandem. More than 95% of survey respondents said that through their participation with Be Your Best, they 'very much' or 'quite a bit' recognize that a collective process can take more time than an individual action. For some people, this can be frustrating. Also, casual and sporadic participation makes it difficult to track progress, provide continual and up-to-date context, and capture past efforts/conversations/evaluations in nuanced detail, resulting in wide gaps in — or the potential for a complete lack of — institutional memory.

Interviewees newer to the work or who hadn't been involved in a while found it hard to pinpoint specific achievements. "At times it has been challenging to keep track of the changes on long-term community projects," said one person.

Still, everyone we spoke with was able to identify in broad brush-strokes the importance of the network. Said one person,

Be Your Best has helped our community make great progress by engaging the many positive organizations and activities so that we all have a better idea of the many resources and people with whom we can connect to get things done. We are fortunate to have BYB as a collaborative organizing group, keeping all of us connected and in touch.

Another echoed, "It's a huge opportunity when people can come together and everybody brings something to the table. The power of people is incredible!"

At the same time, we heard from many that the underlying emphasis on collective action is attractive. According to one interviewee, "Collaboration is very powerful. Sitting together with people who make things happen and working on solutions builds community."

Significance

This finding came as no surprise as the chaotic nature of collaboration has been an issue since Be Your Best formed in 2013. Clarity around what BYB actually is and has capacity to do might help boost engagement and ownership by participating community builders.

Possible Responses

Adjustments

◆ Consider adjusting current meeting format and frequency, scheduling large group meetings every other month or once per quarter, and creating space for more substantive discussions/conversations with workgroups/topic groups/active initiatives meeting more frequently as needed.

New Strategies

◆ Offer collaborative learning and skill-building opportunities to build community and individual capacity (vs. actual project management/CHIP/topic area work).

Experiments

◆ Create space on BYB website or other widely accessible electronic platform for sharing information and opportunities and housing archives of skill-building trainings, links to resources, and relevant community initiatives (history, actions taken, meeting minutes, etc.).

Finding 4: Information is shared currency.

Key Insight: Communication — between and among Be Your Best participants — is central to laying a foundation for trust building, learning, and personal and professional growth.

Across the board, people surveyed said they really value the sharing of information fostered by Be Your Best. They like hearing about other projects and the work that is going on in the community, and they like learning about opportunities for how they can help.

One person described the information sharing that happens through Be Your Best as "inspiring"; another said, "hearing all of the ideas people have, and things they are doing, is exciting." At the same time, several people said that too much time at monthly meetings is spent on superficial roundtable updates and that not all topics covered are relevant to all attendees. Some (sheepishly) admitted that they like virtual meetings because they can "attend" with cameras and audio off and work on/do something else if the conversation doesn't feel applicable.

Survey results corroborate this finding: Through participation in Be Your Best, well over 90% of respondents said they 'very much' understand that information sharing and transparency are key to successful collaboration (see Figure 3).

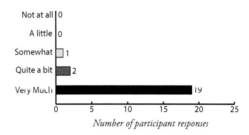

Figure 3. Through my participation in Be Your Best, I better understand that information sharing and transparency are key to successful collaboration. (n=22)

Number of participant responses

Even if people aren't fully engaged, they said they appreciate the opportunities generated from all the information shared through various Be Your Best channels. "I check in with community partners when something they are doing (that I hear about through BYB) makes me curious," said one interviewee. "It opens the door to conversation without cold calling."

Another person noted: "It's a powerful thing to have community connections. Even when I'm mostly listening in, almost inevitably, the information becomes useful."

Significance

It was encouraging to learn from the data that Be Your Best is a relevant resource to help get the word out and connect with others. Network participants clearly value communication and information sharing — the more the better! A critical review of current methods of communication/information sharing will reveal additional opportunities for improvement and curation, which in turn, can enhance utility for network participants.

Possible Responses

Adjustments

- Alter meeting format, specifically regarding roundtable and information sharing. Consider different formats for reporting out and utilize in-person meetings for more substantive discussions/conversations.
- Adjust the frequency and content of meetings. For example: Large group meets every other month while workgroups/topic groups/active initiative groups meet on a more frequent basis as needed.
- Code email info sharing according to category and/or level of urgency.

New Strategies

- Create a weekly email newsletter with categories featuring, for example, opportunities for funding, networking, responding to issues/calls to action, etc., and that links to a website that offers more detailed information on each item.

Experiments

- Build an electronic platform where people can freely connect and share opportunities and access background information.

Finding 5: Connection, Community Building, and Collaboration

Key Insight: Be Your Best is truly one-of-a-kind, offering opportunities that foster meeting new people, building relationships, and connecting to the network and the community — all essential ingredients for effective collaboration and powerful impact.

Surveys and interviews show that participants highly value the relationships and connections made through Be Your Best. Everyone enthusiastically expressed how motivating it was to work toward common goals with others who care about the health and wellbeing of the broader community. "To do the heart work and continue to be inspired, you have to be around people who also love that work," said one person. "The passion for the heart work (in BYB) is inspiring."

In interviews, people said they felt supported by the network in their individual efforts. "Because I was involved with Be Your Best, I felt like our program was attached to the wellbeing of the entire community," commented one person. "The connections made a huge difference in so many ways for us to grow our program."

We also heard during interviews that Be Your Best is an important resource for community building and does a good job of modeling collective principles. As one person put it: "It feels good standing shoulder to shoulder with your allies and friends who you will see later at the grocery store."

All also agreed that relationships underpin collaboration. "Partnerships outweigh the concerns about who is providing the services," said one long-time participant. "We're all working for what's best in the community. At the end of the day, that's what really matters."

Quantitative survey responses reflected much of the same, with 100% of those surveyed saying that since being involved with the network, they are 'very much' or 'quite a bit' more likely to bring an issue or idea to Be Your Best for collaborative partnership (see Figure 4, next page).

Significance

It was encouraging to hear that the original intention for Be Your Best is still one of the main reasons people stay connected to the group and bring others in as well. The collaborative work that happens through Be Your Best has driven a number of critical community efforts, either directly or by example.

Figure 4. Through my participation in Be Your Best, I am more likely to bring an issue or idea to Be Your Best for collabrative partnership. (n=22)

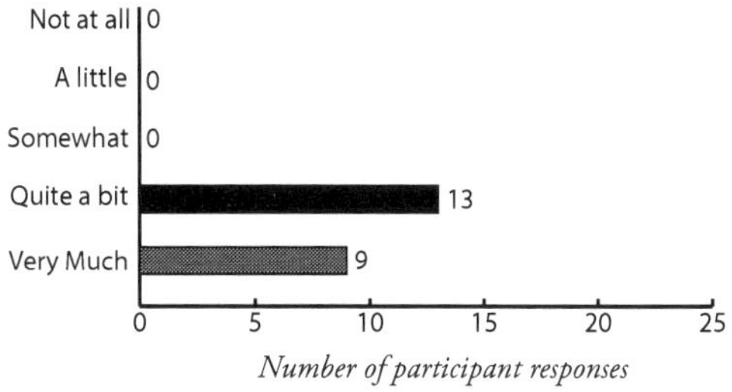

Number of participant responses

Possible Responses

Adjustments

◆ Offer more opportunities for idea sharing, networking, and generally connecting people.

New Strategies

◆ Consider and implement new methods for how meetings are conducted to increase space for deeper connection, more substantive discussions, and how to take action along with opportunities for more targeted personal/professional growth.

Experiments

◆ Actively manage/lead a collaborative project.

Conclusion

Insights Into Impact

The timing of this survey could not have been more appropriate. Since the beginning of the year, a dozen Be Your Best advocates have been discussing how to formally (and sustainably) operationalize what has been, until now, a limited-capacity shape-shifting ad-hoc network of community builders. We have been trying to identify what attracts people to — and keeps them engaged in — collaborative efforts, what elements of the work feel meaningful and supportive, and how we can do better.

The survey and interviews were enormously helpful. We learned that people consider Be Your Best to be a vital community connector and resource and that they appreciate the relationships, information sharing, open communication, creative problem-solving, and opportunities for personal and professional growth that the network engenders. We also heard, loud and clear, that collaborating across sectors with community and equity in the center is hard, can create misunderstandings and breaches of trust, and requires considerable and thoughtful support and skill-building. The evaluation also validated something we already knew: There is room for improvement in how we articulate what Be Your Best is and does and why it matters.

Steps Forward

We will use the results of this evaluation to help us create an operational framework that both leverages Be Your Best's minimal financial resources and maximizes impact for participants, so we can carry on, in an enduring way, the originally envisioned work of better aligning efforts to improve the health and wellbeing of our community. We will do this over the next year by:

- Implementing new methods for how, and how often, meetings are conducted to increase space for deeper connection, more substantive discussions, and ways to take action, along with opportunities for more targeted personal/professional growth. We may, for example, schedule large group meetings every other month or once per quarter with workgroups/topic groups/active initiatives meeting more frequently as needed. We also will build into meetings time and methods for process checking, debriefing, sharing results, and celebrating.

- Tapping ambassadors to recruit executive- and county- and state-level individuals to engage with the broader BYB network on a regular basis and identifying individuals who have the credibility to take leadership and lift up issues/barriers, etc.
- Offering collaborative learning and skill-building opportunities to build community and individual capacity.
- Building a widely accessible electronic platform (i.e., website, Slack channel, bulletin board) where people can freely connect. The electronic platform will also serve as a broad Be Your Best archive with, among other things, links to resources and opportunities, skill-building trainings, and background and updates on community initiatives.

Opportunities for Future Evaluation

Once we have implemented the changes to our operations outlined above, we will conduct another improved evaluation of Be Your Best.

We also hope to build into the work of Be Your Best a more structured, regular, and shared method of evaluating impact.

Burrito Brigade

Waste to Taste

Liz Hurkes, Rene Kane, Kathy Calise, Jen Denson

Organization and Program Overview

Burrito Brigade is a grassroots organization that started in 2014 when the founders realized that Saturdays and Sundays were two of the most food insecure days for people who are unhoused, and the group started making and handing out hundreds of vegan burritos every weekend. Burrito Brigade has since grown to include Little Free Pantries and Waste to Taste. The mission of Burrito Brigade's three projects is to increase food security while decreasing food waste in our communities. Burrito Brigade does this by rescuing consumable food from local grocery stores, restaurants, bakeries, farms, and other organizations that would otherwise end up in the landfill and distributing it directly to individuals, doing so with dignity and without barriers. Burrito Brigade hand-delivers burritos Saturday and Sunday, stocks food in the Little Free Pantries, and provides groceries at the Waste to Taste food hub. Burrito Brigade believes that food is a human right and knows there is enough supply to feed all Oregonians.

In March 2020, Waste to Taste started and quickly became Burrito Brigade's largest program. Waste to Taste is a non-traditional, no-barrier food bank that redirects consumable food that would otherwise end up in a landfill directly to individuals experiencing food insecurity. Waste to Taste fills a need for households that may not qualify for food assistance, those who receive insufficient food assistance, and to low-income households. The program focuses on dignifying the shopping experience by not asking any questions and by letting shoppers create their own food boxes, empowering them to make their own food choices and further reducing food waste. There is an enormous amount of food waste in Eugene, and Waste to Taste is making only a small dent. Waste to Taste rescues approximately 5,000 pounds of food every week, meaning as of September 2022 that we have rescued approximately 600,000 pounds of food since we started. As of September 2022, we have served approximately 18,000 food boxes.

Intended Impact

- **Individuals and families who use Waste to Taste are more food secure:** The food people get from Waste to Taste enables them to augment other systems of support (WIC, SNAP, or other) or their household's ability to purchase food. They have a sense of having enough food to feed themselves and their families without compromising their ability to provide for other essential needs (housing, transportation, health/medical, childcare, education, etc.).

- **People are empowered to make their own food choices:** Waste to Taste shoppers have better access to more fresh fruits and vegetables and food that might be otherwise cost prohibitive. Fresh vegetables and fruit are often expensive, and Waste to Taste makes fresh fruit/vegetables more accessible. Some foods offered at Waste to Taste might be new to our shoppers, and because it's free, there's less risk to try something new, e.g., Maitake mushrooms, pomelo, Beyond Meat, rice flour, etc.

- **Our community is more aware of food waste and food rescue.** People who shop, volunteer, or work with Waste to Taste become advocates for food waste reduction and food rescue in their own household and in the community: Waste to Taste shoppers, volunteers, and partners recognize the impact of Waste to Taste's work to rescue food from the waste stream (pounds rescued and redistributed), their individual or business role in reducing food waste, and their ability to effectively use or redistribute rescued food (our educational component) as well as advocate for food waste reduction/rescue.

Evaluation Methodology

The aim of our evaluation was to see what kind and quality of impact Waste to Taste is having on community members who are food insecure. To understand this, we explored two broad evaluation questions:

1. What kind and quality of impact does Waste to Taste have on participants?
2. What aspects of Waste to Taste are causing this impact?

Over the course of the project, we (a) developed and refined our ideas of intended impact and indicators, (b) designed and implemented a mixed methods outcome evaluation using both qualitative and quantitative means to collect and analyze data, (c) identified themes and findings, and (d) considered the implications to those findings for program improvement and innovation.

This project began by identifying and clarifying the intended impact of Waste to Taste. Once the ideas of impact had been developed, we used the Heart Triangle™ model to identify qualitative and quantitative indicators of impact on the mental, behavioral, and emotional changes in our participants. We used these indicators to design a qualitative interview protocol and a quantitative questionnaire to evaluate progress toward achieving our intended impact.

The Burrito Brigade Project Impact team was assisted by Ash Martins and Sarah Zimmerman.

Qualitative Data Collection and Analysis

For the qualitative portion of the evaluation, we designed an in-depth interview protocol to gain data about the structural, qualitative changes resulting from our program. Our population size for this evaluation was 200+ households (not all households use Waste to Taste regularly). We used a purposeful stratified sampling technique to select a representative sample from the population we serve, including diversity across age and housing status. Since we don't require demographic information from Waste to Taste participants, we based our interviewee selection on our experience and knowledge serving them. Our sample size was 20, drawn from the following strata of our population:

◆ Age
◆ Housing make-up

Our interview team consisted of Jennifer Denson, Sarah Zimmerman, and Rene Kane. We conducted one-on-one interviews lasting from between 15 minutes and one hour in length and collected interview data using handwritten notes, voice recording, and the Otter voice-to-text transcription app.

We then analyzed the data inductively using a modified version of thematic analysis. Each interviewer analyzed the data from their interviews individually to identify initial themes. Together, we developed common themes from all of the interviews collectively. We identified the overarching and inter-interview themes that emerged from the full scope of our data analysis to illuminate the collective insights and discoveries. We mapped these themes visually and examined the dynamics among the themes, causes and catalysts of the themes, new or surprising insights related to the themes, and relationships between the themes that were revealed in the data. We then determined the most significant and meaningful discoveries and brought them forward as findings.

Quantitative Data Collection and Analysis

For the quantitative portion of the evaluation, we designed a questionnaire to collect data on our quantitative indicators of impact. We made this instrument available to all of our participants via a link in the sign-up site. Waste to Taste serves roughly 200 households weekly. We received

84 responses, an approximately 42% response rate. The data were analyzed primarily using measures of central tendency. We identified key insights, patterns, and gaps within the data and incorporated these discoveries into the related findings. The most significant insights from the quantitative data are described in the following narrative.

Limitations

The evaluation was conducted during the COVID-19 pandemic. During the data collection stage, the country was in the midst of the COVID-19 pandemic. This may have resulted in several limitations, including smaller qualitative and quantitative sample sizes than originally intended.

It's likely that not all participants were aware of the online survey. Quantitative survey responses were sought via an email list of participants and on the online appointment sign-up page. If participants weren't using Waste to Taste during that time period, they wouldn't have access to the survey. Likewise, the online survey was inaccessible for Waste to Taste participants who don't use a computer or have limited access to the internet.

Findings

Finding 1: Well-being

Key Insight: Through using Waste to Taste, participants experienced greater well-being in their daily lives.

Well-being can mean different things to different people, and we found that a common thread across interviewees was feeling less stress, less worry, and less burden about procuring and preparing food. One parent said,

> [Waste to Taste has] given us a huge boost to be able to have … an extra bag of groceries … and I've been able to be really creative with the things that I make at home and just stock my pantry, which is just really reassuring.

This led to a general sense of feeling more relaxed and having more emotional energy, such as for this mother who said,

The budget of my own personal time; it's one less meal that I have to prepare a week because I just bring stuff home. And it's kind of like a grab-and-go; everybody grabs what looks good or fun to them, especially if I bring home a pizza. And so, for my time budget, my emotional budget, it's been a huge, huge weight off of my shoulders.

When asked about her family's future, another mother said, "It's helped us come from the low to the high and we're on an upward swing and this was a huge impact."

Interviewees mentioned an increase in creativity and gratitude from receiving higher quality and a greater variety of food. Parents mentioned that they cook and eat together more as a family, and one family has turned the Waste to Taste food boxes into their own family version of the tv show Chopped. Other participants' children are learning new cooking skills, about new foods, and about food waste in general. A participant whose partner is recovering from spinal surgery is now eating more and enough food with the ease of having some high-quality convenience food available for when they have no energy to prepare a meal. An interviewee on food stamps said that he is no longer hungry and is astonished by the quality of food that he now eats. When asked about his future, he also said,

Whenever someone helps me out, I think of it in terms of kind of like a springboard. It's going to take me to something else, like a goal in my life. You know, I have business ideas, I have art ideas, I have all sorts of things that I want to do for my life, and I want to keep making my life better. And whenever someone helps me out, I'm trying to think of how I can use that to get me to these other places; to my goals.

A couple of participants talked about how their children can now participate in activities that had previously been unaffordable with their food budget. Some participants mentioned feeling good that they are not just getting free food, but helping the environment, making their experience more meaningful.

During the qualitative interviews, it became apparent that many Waste to Taste participants experienced significant improvement in their overall well-being ranging from improvements to their household finances, more family cohesion around meals and food, better physical and psychosocial health, and a greater sense of self-sufficiency.

Interview results were corroborated by data gathered in the quantitative survey, where a remarkable 94% of respondents agreed with the statement, "My family's overall well-being had improved since we started shopping at Waste to Taste." Sixty-seven percent of respondents noted a significant decrease in the number of days they did not have enough food to eat. Participants also noted being able to eat healthier and more consistently and an increase in the variety and new types of food they have tried.

Significance

When people experience food insecurity, their well-being can deteriorate for a myriad of reasons. People might feel more anxious and stressed from worrying about procuring food. They might feel more depressed or down with thoughts of not being able to provide for their families. Their sleep might be affected, and their mental and physical health could decrease from all of the above plus a lower quality diet.

We found through the data that participants' sense of well-being had improved with an increase in food, furthering them along their journey in a more whole way. The data shows that participants are experiencing a higher quality of life with less stress, more peace of mind, and better physical and emotional health. Families are more cohesive by being able to cook together and enjoy each other more. Mothers are less burdened and can provide for their families with less emotional toll.

Waste to Taste provides higher quality food than what participants are used to, which increases self-worth and excitement about food. Participants are being connected to food in a different way, and it is trickling out into the rest of their lives.

Finding 2: Feeling Seen

Key Insight: Honoring people's food choices and having no barriers makes participants feel seen, affirmed, and welcomed.

With Waste to Taste, people have the ability to choose exactly what they want, honoring dietary preferences and lifestyles. There is no judgment or shaming of what people decide to put in their box and no barriers to procuring food. One participant shared the most eye-opening thing about Waste to Taste, saying,

> *Not having to qualify in any way, and then I just come in, and I get to make the decisions about what comes home for us and what stays around for somebody else who might be able to use it. I love that. I love it.*

Participants feel welcomed as they are with no barriers to receiving services and with having their choices honored. Another participant described it as an eye-opening experience, saying,

> *The friendliness of everybody. I mean, there were a couple people that said, "Thank you for shopping here." And I thought, well, for anything to say, you're giving us food, and you're thanking me for shopping here?*

Another participant mentioned feeling less anxiety about procuring a food box, knowing that there are no forms to fill out or questions that they need to answer in order to get a box.

Families can better accommodate dietary choices such as veganism, being gluten-free, and eating kosher. One participant said,

> *I have a kosher diet, and I see kosher things that I don't even see in grocery stores. I'm like, wow, that is amazing. And some of the other stuff that seems thoughtful, not even food stuff, like sometimes laundry detergent, and just little things that just come in handy that are really interesting.*

One mother's son adopted vegetarianism at the start of the pandemic, and now they are able to experiment with meat-free foods that are otherwise cost-prohibitive. Another participant's mother and sister are gluten-free, and she is now able to cook a larger variety of foods for them. A different participant further expounded on this by saying,

I eat a certain way. I don't eat processed foods. I'm gluten intolerant, so when I first started needing [food boxes], I was getting federally sponsored boxes. I was getting sick from the food. And I tried for a little bit, you know, but I really did notice that I was getting sick because it's all full of chemicals, fillers, and sugar, like sugar like you can't believe, and fat and just everything that's bad for you. So, I was getting sick by trying to eat that food. So to be able to have this resource where I can get things that I can try and just start from the ground up is incredible.

Shoppers appreciate the ability to satisfy a sweet tooth if so desired, rounding out their food box to represent the whole of a person. Latino participants appreciate having cultural foods available, and everyone across the interviews appreciates the ability to take home and prepare exactly what they want.

Results of the survey corroborate findings from interviews and reinforce that the Waste to Taste program serves all shoppers, all tastes, and all needs. Specifically, 75% of respondents with dietary restrictions or preferences in their family said they were 'always' or 'often' able to find foods that suit their needs (see Figure 1). In their comments, survey respondents indicated a few specialty items that would meet their dietary preferences or household needs, including staples such as cooking oil, bouillons, condiments, frozen fruit, juices, fish, Toby's tofu pate, canned meats; specialty items to accommodate food allergies; and household supplies such as toilet paper, diapers, food wrap.

Figure 1. Since we started shopping at Waste to Taste, members of my family with dietary restrictions or preferences have been more able to get foods that suite their needs. (n=53)

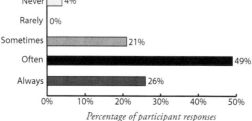

Percentage of participant responses

It's worth observing that the average demographics of Waste to Taste users reveal that many are above the income limits for social services such as SNAP, and/or they do not have children and therefore do not qualify for programs like WIC or TANF to supplement their food needs. It stands to reason that Waste to Taste is meeting community needs that would otherwise go unaddressed, based on income criteria, household size, number of children, etc.

Significance

Traditional food banks have a tendency to cause anxiety amongst participants with required questions, forms, and qualifiers and have a tendency to give out predetermined food that participants do not want. This can cause some people to not use food banks at all, can make others feel unseen, especially when it comes to cultural food choices, and further contributes to food waste when unwanted food goes unused. Just because a person is food insecure does not mean that they do not have preferences.

Waste to Taste sees people for who they are and where they are, and we found that that matters. When people get to choose exactly what they want, and from a high-quality selection, they feel seen, valued, and empowered. This is especially important for Latino participants wanting to find cultural foods and for those with different dietary needs and lifestyles.

All of this leads to people going home with exactly what they want, which also further reduces food waste in our community from a decrease in thrown-out, unwanted food. People are more likely to use Waste to Taste for these reasons, as well as the fact that they are not asked a single qualifying question because Burrito Brigade believes that food is a basic human right.

Finding 3: Eating more variety

Key Insight: Shoppers are eating a greater variety of food and more fruits and vegetables, which otherwise were cost prohibitive.

Fresh produce, especially organic produce, as well as other cost-prohibitive items such as fancy meats, cheeses, mushrooms, and other unusual offerings, i.e., Beyond Meat, can be out of reach to food insecure families. Throughout our interviews, shoppers felt excited to try new things and to discover new favorite foods and appreciated having accessibility to things that they never would have otherwise tried because of cost. Participants were shocked at the high-quality food that they got to choose from and appalled that it was meant to be wasted.

One participant was astonished at the amount and type of stuff that supermarkets throw away, saying, "I cannot believe the stuff that we get here that I'm not able to access." Another participant talked about getting excited about cooking with fresh produce again, especially greens, which were previously cost-prohibitive.

Participants indicated their creativity is heightened when they bring home different and new foods every week and expressed appreciation for the surprise of what they might find. Some shoppers have found that they are doing more scratch cooking than they were before Waste to Taste and cooking more in general without a reliance on instant food.

Some new favorite foods mentioned by Waste to Taste participants included mushrooms, heirloom tomatoes, Trader Joe's salads, fennel, arugula, chard, pomelos, and jicama taco shells. One participant who procures and prepares food for her picky neighbor said, "He loves [pomelos] and for him to like something different is gigantic." Another participant, shocked at the variety, said,

Just coming in here and seeing that this isn't even Food For Lane County that gets all this excess food, like, this is even left over after that. And I'm really stunned by that because there are so many people that are hungry, and I just can't believe this is happening. So I think that's been a shock to me that there's so much food that we don't get because we don't have access to it.

Results of the quantitative survey echo those of the interviews. A slight majority (59%) of respondents indicated they were eating a greater variety of foods since shopping at Waste to Taste (see Figure 2). Of those who said the variety of foods they were eating had increased, many noted they are able to eat healthier and more consistently and that they are able to try new foods and have a greater variety of foods to choose from. Participants described eating new vegetables, trying new prepared foods (e.g., packaged jicama or pre-made deli foods such as salads), new brands, types of milk or cheese, and vegan products.

Figure 2. Since we started shopping at Waste to Taste, the variety of foods we eat has increased. (n=82)

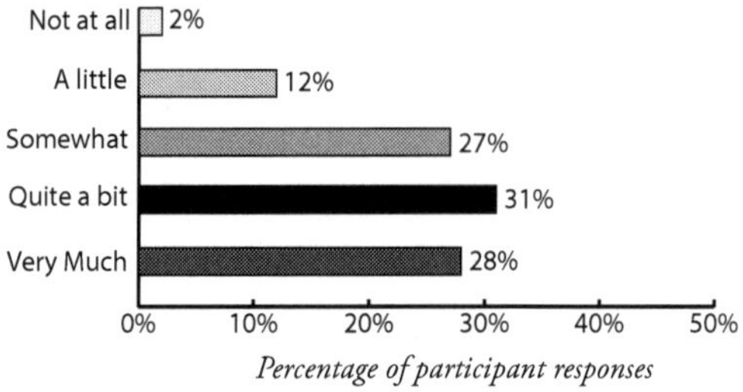

Percentage of participant responses

Significance

While eating a variety of good food is a privileged simple pleasure to some, it is unobtainable and/or cost prohibitive to others. Waste to Taste participants discovered a greater enjoyment of food with a variety of higher quality options, leading them to try new things and expand their palettes. This variety included not only access to fresh, organic produce but also meats, cheeses, and prepackaged foods that cater to vegan and gluten-free diets. This led to a more expansive perspective and deeper appreciation of food with the knowledge of the kind and quality of food that is out there that would have gone to waste.

Some participants with restrictive diets were eating less variety with diet appropriate foods being out of budget or not offered at traditional food banks. Their diets have become more well-rounded with the variety now available to them at Waste to Taste. To the more privileged, eating a variety of food is the spice of life, and Waste to Taste wants that to be available to all.

Finding 4: Environmentalism

Key Insight: Waste to Taste shoppers have become more aware of and active in the reduction of food waste.

Participants across the board were shocked when they learned that all of the food at Waste to Taste was destined for a landfill. Much of the food at Waste to Taste is either "imperfect" or "expired" but perfectly consumable. When asked about what was most surprising about learning about food waste, one participant said,

The number of things that get rejected – just the sheer quantity of it. It surprises me that some of the prepared things, like some of the salad kits - they're perfect, there's not a blemish on them – but they're here because there's a "sell by" date. The "sell by" date is probably good to some degree, but there's an awful lot of food that's wasted because of it.

Some participants knew about the problem of food waste generally but did not know the extent of it before shopping at Waste to Taste. Shoppers have learned that they can cut off an "imperfection" if needed and salvage what they can. One participant talked about how much more aware he has become about the life cycle of food and the energy that is needed for every step of the cycle. Some participants acknowledged that they sometimes take food that they normally wouldn't be interested in just to help reduce food from going to waste.

Other participants feel even more of a responsibility to utilize everything they get from Waste to Taste, knowing that it was destined for the landfill. One participant said that she is less lazy when it comes to cooking because of an all of a sudden moralistic standpoint to prepare what she gets from Waste to Taste. Another participant said about their household,

I think we're all pretty stoked to be participating and reducing food waste. And a lot of times, if there's a bunch of something, I like to take it home to process it like using up or taking a box of apples to press and making cider, or a bucket of plums to make a jam. And then that's my

jam for the year. And yeah, doing things like that is really helpful and feels really good, especially during the harvest season when there's so many tomatoes and so much fruit that people don't know what to do with it. Definitely feels good to take it home and process it. Make sure that it doesn't go to waste.

Parents are educating their children on the importance of reducing food waste and how it helps the environment. One mother said, "My son is learning to not let things go to waste. Like he doesn't fully understand it, but he knows I come here every week to get food, and he can help me make stuff from what I get here. So, he's learning how to cook and do things with me."

Customers are telling their friends and family about Waste to Taste as not just a place to get good, free food but also as a place to make a positive impact on the environment. One example is this participant who said,

It has me thinking about my personal community, just in terms of reaching out to my friends who might need this as a resource or care about food going into the landfill and being able to stop that from happening. And so, a family's benefited by helping pad their budget a little bit, and then we're able to make a bigger impact on the environment as well.

Of those who took the survey, slightly under half (49%) indicated a significant change ('A lot,' 'Quite a bit') in their thinking about food waste, with another 27% saying their thinking had somewhat changed. A slightly higher percentage (55%) indicated a significant increase in their family's awareness of their own household food waste.

In some cases, awareness meant knowing the food at Waste to Taste would have been headed to the landfill, as reflected in these comments:

As a country I know how thoroughly wasteful we are. When I learned about economics and how they would just destroy crops to create scarcity and drive-up prices in high school...It f-ing floored me. We'd rather make a profit than feed those in need.

I think of just how much food gets tossed from local groceries and restaurants and it's really sad.

Other comments described how participants' personal practices had been informed:

I love being able to enjoy free food that stores, and restaurants consider not acceptable, but in actuality still has some life left in them! It's like being given a second chance!!!

Freezing for future use and making new leftover meals.

I am trying to learn how to change up leftovers to make new meals.

Lastly, this comment recognized the circular nature of Waste to Taste:

I love that W2T sends things to pig farmers.

Twenty-four percent of the respondents taking the survey showed no or only a little change in their thinking around food waste. This indicates to the organization that there is still much work to be done to enhance participants' knowledge of what they can do to prevent food waste and its importance.

Significance

Food waste is estimated to be roughly 35% of the total food supply and has many negative downstream effects beyond hunger and food insecurity. Food decomposing in landfills increases local greenhouse gas emissions; water, oil, and other resources that go into producing and transporting food are wasted; and biodiversity decreases from a loss of habitat. Waste to Taste participants had knowledge of food waste to varying degrees before Waste to Taste, but all were shocked to see how much food was destined for the landfill firsthand. They became not just consumers but also active participants in reducing food waste. Beyond taking home food, they have become food waste advocates in their homes and neighborhoods, have become more creative with how to use food to further prevent waste, and are realizing their own individual impacts on the environment. Reducing food waste is just one component of fighting climate change, and the Waste to Taste community is doing its part.

Finding 5: Financial Relief

Key Insight: We found that participants' food expenditures were reduced or negated entirely, allowing families to allocate those funds to other necessities and reducing financial stress and anxiety.

Some participants still go to the grocery store for specific things that they cannot find at Waste to Taste but are spending less than they normally would. Families plan their grocery shopping and meal plan around going to Waste to Taste first to make sure they're saving the most money and that everything gets used.

One participant's household food bill has been cut by at least $350, alleviating financial stress while their partner is convalescing from surgery. One mother's monthly food bill has decreased by $200-$300. Another family doesn't have a food bill at all anymore because they only shop at Waste to Taste. That mother also noted,

I had a major failing of the system in my house, that we put water all over the place, and it's a $3,300 repair. And that is money I didn't have. And I'm working extra to make it up, but at least I don't have to worry about [feeding us], which is everything. It's just everything. And I woke up this morning knowing I was coming here today and knowing that [Waste to Taste] is consistent, and it's there, and it's reliable has made everything else as hard as it has been easier.

Another participant has been able to contribute more to her emergency fund, saying, "Even when we get a gallon of milk, that gives me that kind of money that I can put toward my emergency fund [for] when things are going bad or when I have to get hearing aids, things like that so I could stash that money."

Others are putting more towards other bills. One person's father now has more gas money to travel back and forth to California to visit his other grandchildren, and another participant is able to put more money towards her gas tank as well. A participant who also uses food stamps now has more wiggle room and rollover with his food stamp benefits. One vegan participant had to retire because of COVID-19, even though she wasn't quite eligible for social security. She now goes to the grocery store twice a month instead of twice a week and feels much less stressed about her finances. She also said, "The difference is night and day. I don't know how I would have made it, because most of our money right now is going to pay for things other than food [and now we've] paid some bills that we wouldn't have been able to pay otherwise."

Participants feel that they can experience a little bit of luxury by eating some prepared foods that they could never afford, splurging on eating out on occasion, and having more time for themselves. One shared, "This is my time, but time doesn't mean I have to make the money to spend the money. And so, there's just been a little bit of lightness there even while getting free food."

Results of the quantitative survey corroborate the quantitative survey, with 68% of the respondents indicating that shopping at Waste to Taste impacted their household budget 'very much' or 'quite a bit' (see Figure 3 on next page). Respondents noted a positive impact on their finances in a variety of ways, including:

- Saving money
- Being able to afford essentials such as gasoline for their cars
- Being able to afford "extras" around the house
- Being able to catch up on non-food-related bills and/or plan for the future

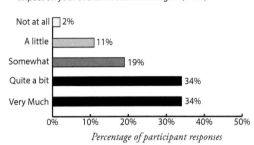

Figure 3. Since you've been shopping at Waste to Taste, have you seen an impact on your overall household budget? (n=83)

Percentage of participant responses

A sampling of family finance-related responses to the question "Since you've been shopping at Waste to Taste, what has your family been able to do now that you weren't able to do before?" include:

We have been able to save/pay for needed repairs to our home and vehicles. Additionally, we can prioritize our health and make better meal choices.

[I can] afford to feed my growing family without running out of our grocery budget before [the] end of month.

We eat well, fresh veggies, eggs, bread, meat are now available and not out of reach due to price.

Pay medical bills, have a little extra money for gifts and birthdays for the kids.

Eat things that I could not afford or brands I didn't know about.

Significance

Economic disparity has always existed in this country, but the pandemic reversed any progress being made in poverty levels, and the issue is being perpetuated and exacerbated for people living with low/fixed incomes who are also now stressed by rising living costs, gas prices, and inflation. Waste to Taste found that this is no longer just an issue for those living with low incomes but that it is also bleeding into higher income levels. Everyone that W2T serves is feeling strapped, even across what would traditionally be thought of as middle-income levels.

Participants reported feeling some financial relief due to the reduced amount of money that they spend on food, sometimes wiping out the food bill altogether. They are able to have a larger amount of discretionary income, and some have started or been contributing more to their emergency funds. People are more able to pay their bills and be more flexible with their budgets. Participants are feeling less stress about their financial burdens, increasing their levels of well-being. Waste to Taste alone will not relieve all the financial burden that people are currently feeling, but Waste to Taste is making a dent, and participants are grateful for it.

Finding 6: Frustration

Key Insight: Even with Waste to Taste, some customers still experience some frustration and uncertainty with procuring food.

Inflation is driving food prices and other expenses up, making things that cannot be procured at Waste to Taste more expensive. Some participants vocalized fear of Waste to Taste someday going away or contending with long lines and food shortages, such as this participant who said, "I just hope this doesn't end now that COVID's ending because it's made a big difference."

One participant voiced frustration over how expensive groceries are now, coupled with the shock of how much actually gets thrown out. Other participants say that when they go to other more traditional food banks that they get food that they do not want. One Latino participant said (translated),

Other resources give boxes that are already made up. And most of the time, they're foods that are chosen for me or prepared in some way or packaged, and we don't eat any of those things. But now that my husband is working again, we can buy what we can't get here. But we can't use most things that we would get from a school or other sources, so those are the frustrations. I want to be able to choose myself because I'm the one that does all of the food preparation.

Although Waste to Taste regularly includes fresh produce, one participant said that it could sometimes be hit and miss, meaning that they might have to go without something for the week. Another participant is frustrated with how expensive it is to eat healthily but is now eating more healthy foods that she procures from Waste to Taste.

Even though some participants are cooking more, others find it hard to cook from scratch after working and appreciate the option of higher quality convenience foods that they wouldn't get at other food banks. When asked what she still finds frustrating about procuring food, one participant said that she no longer feels frustration, saying,

You allow us to adjust without having to check in or that you're not looking over our shoulder has allowed me to relax into the shopping experience or procuring experience because I don't feel what you're doing is trying to regulate me or to control me. And in that way, I am circumspect in what I get. I am looking at what I get and making sure I'm leaving enough things for other people who are going to come through. I don't have to do any explaining or form filling out or anything. It feels like there's trust and generosity in that, and while you also have the structure and guidelines in place, I'm happy to follow them because everything else is just so easy. You make it really, really easy to be poor.

In relation to their Waste to Taste experiences, survey respondents reported relatively little frustration with the availability of food. Seventy-two percent said they were able to get foods they or their family like more regularly since shopping with Waste to Taste 'always' or 'most of the time.'

Significance

While Waste to Taste is clearly making an impact on participants' lives, a single organization can only do so much to address food insecurity. Waste to Taste participants continue to feel financial stress from rising gas prices, inflation, and dealing with higher costs of living, and this stress goes beyond low-income folks to the middle class. Participants who continue to use other food banks experience continued frustration over not being able to choose their own foods. And for some, Waste to Taste seems too good to be true, making them worried that Waste to Taste might someday disappear.

Burrito Brigade is committed to Waste to Taste and has embarked on procuring foundational support to help secure the future of Waste to Taste. Burrito Brigade is also exploring additional food resources and partnering with other organizations to source non-perishable household items. There are many people in our community who need help and do not want to feel the stigma of reaching out for it. Waste to Taste meets people where they are, with no judgments, questions, or proselytizing. Waste to Taste is humanizing the food bank experience and helping the environment at the same time, and people are grateful for it.

Finding 7: Community

Key Insight: Waste to Taste shoppers feel a sense of community at Waste to Taste that spills into their other relationships.

There is awe amongst participants seeing all of the food from the different stores, farms, and bakeries, which increases their sense of having a community that cares for them. Some participants have become volunteers at Waste to Taste, and others would like to when they have more time. Oftentimes in line, shoppers will share information with each other about what something is and how to prepare it.

One participant mentioned how heartwarming it is to see such a community effort, and other participants are inspired when they learn about the involvement of the community. Participants bring things from their own households that they won't use, hoping that someone else will. One participant's feel-good moment is taking food boxes to other people in his complex. A mother doesn't feel her chest constrict anymore when her child's friends come over to hang out because she can now be generous in offering them food.

Participants share their experiences with neighbors, friends, and family and promote Waste to Taste as a community-focused endeavor. One participant said,

> *The second part that neither of us touched on was the community thing. I just wanted to throw in there that it never ceases to amaze me how this is so grassroots. And this is really just community members coming together and making this happen, and like you know, you try to sign up for SNAP benefits or something, which is, of course, a really helpful service for countless people, but it's so bureaucratic, and it's so quantitatively based and [it] just very much perpetuates the disconnection between producer and consumer. And I feel like Waste to Taste is what food justice should be because it's direct, and there isn't bureaucracy. [I]t's just people walking in a lot of the time and being like, "Can I take whatever I want?" Yes. And it's really also changed my perception of what a community is capable of doing without necessarily asking permission or going through a bunch of bureaucratic pathways. They can just organize, and they can stop stuff from going to waste and help people that need access to stuff.*

It's challenging to assess a person's feelings of "community" in a quantitative survey, and it makes sense that very few of those surveyed indicated a greater connection with the W2T community and their local community. However, one comment provided by a person who took the survey tells a different story. They shared,

> *When I get a food box, I often make a big soup or stew using as many of the vegetables and canned goods as I can. I share this with my elderly neighbor. This is also how I cook when I get a CSA box or harvest from my garden.*

Other results from the quantitative survey that might be interpreted as indicating a greater sense of community connection are the increased frequency with which families ate more meals at home (84% reporting a significant increase) and the number of families that said they prepared more meals together since shopping at Waste to Taste (58% reporting a significant increase).

Significance

While we understand (and assume) there may be impacts on people's diets, household finances, and other practical impacts of shopping at Waste to Taste, this intangible impact on the sense of community people have as a result is an added and somewhat surprising outcome.

Having a sense of community is important for psychological health and developing a sense of belonging. Without it, people could feel isolated, disconnected, depressed, and could have feelings of burnout or low self-esteem. Waste to Taste started in March of 2020 when the world shut down in response to COVID-19. It was a time when people needed not only emergency access to food but also needed to maintain some sort of connection to community and a feeling of belonging. The pandemic is not over, and although there has been a relative return to normal, food insecurity still persists due to inflation, a rise in gas prices, and economic disparity that was caused/exacerbated by the pandemic, all of which will be hard to overcome. Life can be difficult, and it can be made a little bit better by belonging to a community and having easy access to food.

The Future: How can Waste to Taste improve or expand its services?

As with most young non-profits, Burrito Brigade/Waste to Taste is operated with minimal staffing and a small budget. The program's capacity to reach more people, provide relevant products and services, and educate Waste to Taste shoppers about the food that is provided, how best to use and store it and how to reduce food waste is frequently limited. Regardless of the limitations, Waste to Taste staff, volunteers, and the Burrito Brigade board are always looking toward improvement and expanding the program's reach and impact.

The qualitative interviews yielded some insight into unmet needs and opportunities, and the following quantitative survey results suggest several areas that the Waste to Taste program might address in the future:

- Increased access to preferred, specialty, cultural, or religious foods
- Access to dessert or special treat items
- Opportunities to discover new foods
- Opportunities to connect with the Waste to Taste and local communities
- Information and resources for starting or expanding home gardens

Programmatic response to these findings might include the following:

Information, education, and outreach:

- Create and maintain a periodic email newsletter to Waste to Taste recipients who opt in. The newsletter could feature all the items below as well as additional community resources for food, family support, etc. (creating community; education).
- Creating and posting (onsite and on social media) educational materials that describe new or unusual foods and how to use them (expanding use of new or unusual foods).
- Creating and posting (onsite and on social media) educational materials that feature available foods and creative ways to use them (e.g., making calzones, frittatas, pizzas, smoothies, etc.)
- A series of social media posts that help Waste to Taste shoppers fully utilize the foods they get from the pantry (increased awareness of food waste and prevention).
- Develop educational pieces for social media and the newsletter on food waste/using foods more effectively and efficiently.
- Conduct quick, on-the-spot surveys with one or two questions and easy ways to respond (sticker on whiteboard). It could be posted in the waiting area. Results posted the following week and/or in the newsletter.
- Recognize new shoppers, so they get special treatment and assistance. Consider providing a "treat" for their first time. Prepare

an informational handout they can take with them - it's a lot of information to absorb!

- Host food preservation workshops (partner with OSU Extension), cooking classes for parents and children, etc.
- Host a cooking class for youth who have just aged out of foster care (coordinate with Community Connect).
- Create handouts specifically for children.

Building community:

- Establish an advisory board of Waste to Taste shoppers that can periodically provide feedback to program staff. Recognize their contribution in the newsletter or social media posts.
- Invite shoppers to submit favorite recipes or tips on using food from Waste to Taste; publish them in the newsletter.
- Publish interviews with Waste to Taste shoppers and feature their use of foods procured from the pantry, describing impacts and benefits to their household, etc. (community and connection).
- Offer a comprehensive resources list (not just food).
- Periodically send information to food sources about their impact.
- Make sure there's a Spanish speaker present at all times.
- Reach out to the BIPOC, immigrant and refugee community.

Sourcing and providing food:

- Where possible, increase the number and variety of sources for food at Waste to Taste, in particular, specialty foods or those to meet specific dietary or religious needs.
- Consider providing staples such as peanut butter, canned fish and meat, soups, etc., on a regular basis to meet the needs of shoppers who may not qualify for food boxes from other organizations.
- Expand the program's ability to store rescued food, e.g., over-ripe bananas are peeled and frozen. Are there other fresh fruits or vegetables that can be treated similarly? Freeze or dehydrate?

On-site and/or facility changes:

- Expand the hours to better accommodate participants' work schedules.
- Have stockers become greeters.
- Have volunteers who staff Waste to Taste familiarize themselves with what new or unique foods are available that day and how to use them.
- Make up meal kits based on the day's food

Conclusion

Insights Into Impact

With our mission being to increase food security while decreasing food waste, Burrito Brigade has always felt that we were making an impact simply by feeding people. As it turns out, our impact is greater and more nuanced with Waste to Taste. We confirmed positive impacts on Waste to Taste participants, who indeed feel more food secure, and also confirmed that they feel more empowered with making their own food choices and are more aware of food waste and food rescue, priding themselves on being part of the solution.

Food security showed up with our participants in that they were simply receiving and eating more food than normal, they were less stressed about budgets in general and about stretching resources at the end of the month, and they are eating a greater variety of foods, including more fresh fruits and vegetables. Parents are more able to pay rent, utilities, and other bills without compromising on feeding their families.

Empowerment with making their own food choices was conveyed by many participants feeling seen with their dietary preferences and having different dietary lifestyles accommodated. Participants appreciate being able to choose foods that they might not have tried before due to expense, broadening their palettes, and increasing food satisfaction. There was also an appreciation of being able to choose exactly what they want, which is unusual at more traditional food banks.

Food waste awareness was proven to have increased, primarily through participants' shock when they first learn that everything presented at Waste to Taste has been rescued. This has sparked some participants to take things that they normally wouldn't, to do better about using everything that they take, and to destigmatize Waste to Taste to friends and family as a way of helping the environment, all in order to decrease food waste.

Steps Forward

As Burrito Brigade expands and as Waste to Taste's capacity to both procure and distribute food increases, it will be important to continually seek out new partnerships for accessing food surplus and to develop new ways to assist Waste to Taste shoppers and to expand our reach.

Through this process, we realized that even though Waste to Taste participants have greater access to higher quality food, some participants experience frustration with their inability to meet specific dietary needs through Waste to Taste, such as a greater variety of proteins. We will work on broadening our partnership with Food for Lane County and other agencies to help fill these gaps.

One of our greatest priorities is moving Waste to Taste (and Burrito Brigade as a whole) into one permanent building. The new location is more centrally located and closer to an LTD bus line, and our hours will be extended, all of which will increase accessibility to a larger number of people. There will be more opportunities to increase outreach in our new building with opportunities to teach cooking and preservation classes. Also of great importance is that with a permanent location, Burrito Brigade will be spending far fewer hours on the logistics of multiple temporary locations and will be able to focus more on expanding our reach and supporting the people we serve. We will also expand our Waste to Taste outreach to include more folks who are transitioning to permanent housing who can be found at places such as Safe Spot camps and Everyone Village.

We had no idea what kind of impact Waste to Taste would have when it began in 2020. Through the research that we conducted during Project Impact, we realized our impact was far greater than we could have imagined.

Opportunities for Future Evaluation

Waste to Taste will utilize the evaluation methodologies learned through Project impact to encourage the Board of Directors to commit the time and resources to an online survey and qualitative interviews on an annual basis or as often as may be needed. Working with our partners to evaluate the relationship with them is important as Waste to Taste expands its partnerships and serves the broader diverse community.

The results of both the online survey and qualitative interviews could be used in short- and long-term strategic planning for Waste to Taste and shared with our donors, volunteers, and participants.

The results of the interviews and online survey provide valuable guidance for the Waste to Taste program - with data and information on where the program has been successful and had a positive impact and where there are gaps the program may be prepared to fill.

Oregon Family Support Network

Oregon Family Support Network

Support and Advocacy

Lisa Butler, Brooke Doster, Alyse Heun, Nita Likes, and Megan Prav

Organization and Program Overview

Oregon Family Support Network is a 501(c)3 nonprofit founded in 1991, which began as a grassroots community organization providing support groups and education to families with a strong advocacy component. Our goal and mission are that every family deserves to be heard and understood.

In our involvement with families and caregivers, we strive to serve those individuals and families who experience complex challenges resulting from mental or behavioral health issues. We help to remove obstacles, including poverty, domestic violence, homelessness, disconnection from family, untreated mental health and addiction, as well as profound traumatic experiences.

Some of our purposes have included:

- Connecting and empowering families in creating positive outcomes for youths experiencing significant behavioral health challenges.
- Assisting families in navigating educational and legal systems to secure needed supports and services as well as providing one-to-one peer support services to any such individuals.
- Recommending and matching families with accessible community resources in their location.

Intended Impact

Intended impacts that were identified at the start of this study were:

1. **Families express their individuality authentically.** Each family is unique, and we commemorate their individual experiences, culture, and worldview. Our support to families is centered around family individuality.

2. **Families are hopeful and confident in the present and for their future.** Families have aspiration and certainty in navigating systems and supports for their family.

3. **Families champion their lived experience as equals with the system.** Families have the courage to speak their truth; they are acknowledged as experts of their lived experience, and they actively impact system change.

Evaluation Methodology

The aim of our evaluation was to see what kind and quality of impact our support and advocacy services are having on the families, youths, and caregivers throughout the state of Oregon. To understand this, we explored two broad evaluation questions:

1. What kind and quality of impact are we having on families and caregivers?
2. What aspects of our program are causing this impact?

Over the course of the project, we (a) developed and refined our ideas of intended impact and indicators, (b) designed and implemented a mixed methods outcome evaluation using both qualitative and quantitative means to collect and analyze data, (c) identified themes and findings, and (d) considered the implications to those findings for program improvement and innovation.

This project began by identifying and clarifying the intended impact of our support and advocacy services. Once the ideas of impact had been developed, we used the Heart Triangle™ model to identify qualitative and quantitative indicators of impact on the mental, behavioral, and emotional changes in our participants. We used these indicators to design a qualitative interview protocol and a quantitative questionnaire to evaluate progress toward achieving our intended impact.

Qualitative Data Collection and Analysis

For the qualitative portion of the evaluation, we designed an in-depth interview protocol to gain data about the structural, qualitative changes resulting from our program. We had delimited our population to families who had recently been involved with our support services in the last year to gain a more accurate understanding of how families are currently being supported and how they are navigating challenges. Our population size for this evaluation was around 200. We used a purposeful stratified sampling technique to select a representative sample from the population we serve. Out of that population, our final sample size ended up being 23 families, which were drawn from the following strata of our population:

- Any family or caregiver who received support from OFSN in the last year.

Our interview team consisted of Alyse Heun (Intake and Referral Coordinator), Nita Likes (EHR Administrator), and Megan Prav (EHR Administrator). We convened one-on-one interviews lasting from between 45 minutes and one hour in length and collected interview data using handwritten notes as well as utilizing Otter.ai, which we used as our voice-to-text transcription service.

We then analyzed the data inductively using a modified version of thematic analysis. Each interviewer analyzed the data from their interviews individually to identify initial themes. Together, we developed common themes from all of the interviews collectively. We identified the overarching and inter-interview themes that emerged from the full scope of our data analysis to illuminate the collective insights and discoveries. We mapped these themes through a qualitative data analysis and examined the dynamics among the themes, causes and catalysts of the themes, new or surprising insights related to the themes, and relationships between the themes that were revealed in the data. We then determined the most significant and meaningful discoveries and brought them forward as findings.

Quantitative Data Collection and Analysis

For the quantitative portion of the evaluation, we designed a questionnaire to collect data on our quantitative indicators of impact. We administered this instrument to roughly 198 families and caregivers. We had responses from 34 families, a 17% response rate. The data were analyzed primarily using measures of central tendency. We identified key insights, patterns, and gaps within the data and incorporated these discoveries into the related findings. The most significant insights from the quantitative data are described in the following narrative.

Limitations

This evaluation was conducted while many of our staff were in transition and experiencing some growing pains. During the data collection stage, this ultimately impacted how many families we were able to reach out to and interview. This may have resulted in several limitations, including a smaller qualitative and quantitative sample size than we had originally hoped for.

Findings

Finding 1: A New Sense of Confidence

Key Insight: Families supported by the work at OFSN increased their confidence within their families and communities.

It is apparent from our interviewees that families have felt a new sense of confidence when showing up as parents. They have expressed feelings of increased confidence in managing conflict and knowing how and when to reach out for support. Here are what a few parents had to say on the matter:

> *I am more willing to reach out for help more so than before. Especially since I know there is all kinds of help out there available. Sometimes it*

takes a long time to get things going and moving. I want to give up and get frustrated. But eventually, patience wins out, and everything works out and comes through.

I attended a lot of support groups; I got to know other people. I took a lot of classes through OFSN and other agencies to understand how to parent my children more effectively. I learned how to talk in a way that other providers could understand while also ensuring that I wasn't giving away what we needed in the process.

This absolutely shows us how families have been able to advocate for themselves and find confidence while accessing support and resources. But on the other side of this, our survey data which gave us a more clinical overview of the factors at work gave us a slightly different picture. For instance, about 32% of respondents reported a more significant increase in their confidence while accessing support and sources, while 35% reported no change. So, there is definitely more that we can explore around this topic.

Throughout our interviews, many families also expressed that they felt an increased sense of personal confidence and explained that they felt they had grown so much from when they first started in their attempts to access support. One individual had said this:

I am learning to embrace and enjoy the journey and how it helps me and my family grow and develop. My confidence is a lot more, thanks to my FSS [Family Support Specialist]. Both of them really helped me use my voice and demand the supports my kids were entitled to.

Other statements made by families in expressing how their confidence has grown since being involved in OFSN include:

I didn't believe in mental health because of the way I was raised; my family support specialist helped me in the work to become more confident in caring for my family's needs and accepting help.

I'm more confident in myself and as a parent.

We were really able to see and corroborate these kinds of statements throughout our quantitative data. We found that 35% of our survey respondents reported that their confidence around expressing themselves authentically has had at least some positive growth, while another 33% reported that they experienced "quite a bit" or "very much" growth in expressing themselves more confidently (see Figure 1).

Figure 1. Since working with OFSN, my confidence in expressing myself authentically has improved. (n=34)

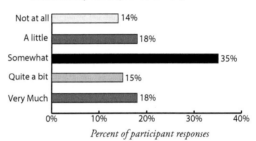

Percent of participant responses

Significance
In order to do the work that is so essential to aiding families, we absolutely need to instill a sense of confidence; that is the essence of our work. Without that confidence, families are not able to preserve and persist through the challenges that they face in daily life. Hearing families express how much of a difference this makes has helped us to recognize how important it is that we continue to build this up for the families that we support.

We also had a perhaps unexpected realization, an ah-ha moment, as it were. We discovered that the parents and caregivers were not only able to share how their confidence had grown as a caregiver but also how their personal confidence in themselves had taken a dramatic turn for the better as well.

Possible Responses
Adjustments
- Reach out deeper into communities to understand their needs.

- Empower families to even further step into their role of being able to vocalize their needs and struggles.

New Strategies
- Additional training on mental health support – for staff.
- Implementing the Family Journey Assessment and monitoring/reflecting on the change families may obtain through their journey with OFSN.

Experiments
- Creating additional trainings for Family Support Specialists on helping build self-sufficiency.
- Increase the marketing of training to families in communities that are not supported by OFSN.

Finding 2: The Beauty of Growth

Key Insight: Families supported by OFSN experienced a sense of growth and unlocked new strengths as parents and caregivers.

Throughout our interviews, it has truly been eye-opening to learn that no matter the circumstances at play or whatever barriers may come against families, there has been a noticeable personal growth in families as they have been empowered to overcome the challenges that they face. They've allowed themselves to grow in their parenting skills, and to break the bonds of the past and learn how to be more effective parents. Even as families are fighting for what they need, they've grown in their own self-advocacy and have less to hold themselves back around their engagement in the system.

One family we interviewed stated,

I discovered that my story and experience is far from extraordinary when it comes to families trying to get the services and support they need for their families. I discovered that I can be brazen and bold when I need to be in order to ensure my kids are getting the best possible life they deserve. I guess I am surprised how much independence and self-sufficiency I have and that I know what I need. I see myself more capable as a parent and able to tell providers what will and won't work for my family. I am also more engaging with my girls and able to listen to them and understand their needs and wants, not just mine.

This really gave us a great outlook and insight on how families have grown so much from their own experiences and to know how to make effective decisions for themselves and their children. It seems that there has really been a growing sense of empowerment at play as well. As we compared this to our survey data, we saw that 35% of respondents reported they had felt "very much" or "quite a bit" more empowered, and another 30% reported feeling at least somewhat empowered (see Figure 2).

Figure 2. Since working with OFSN, my family and I feel more empowered. (n=34)

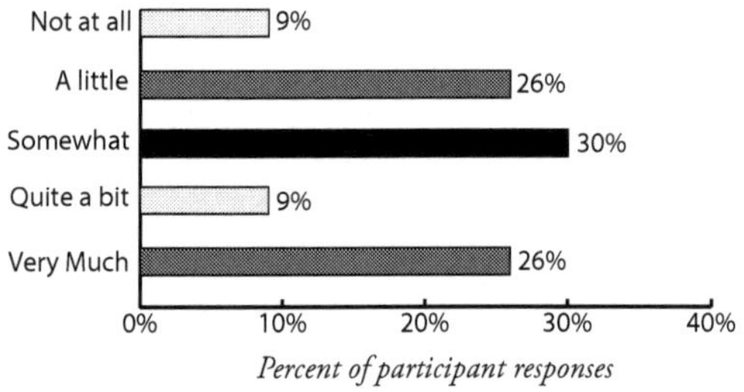

Percent of participant responses

Another family interviewed expressed feeling a new sense of growth, saying:

I learned how to use schedules to set expectations... I have a hard time with conflict, I don't want people upset, so I tend to be more passive when talking to my kids. I learned I can be assertive, and that isn't abusive.

In this case, we could see how being able to set expectations and take a minute to pause allowed this family to grow and show up better for themselves and as a parent. It has been great to see where parents have been able to learn to be more assertive but, at the same time, realize that their actions are not abusive, as this interviewee had stated.

To conclude, a few other quotes that equally spoke to this finding on how that process has looked for other families included:

Last year my son was having a really hard time and getting really bad grades in school, and I felt like they were telling me multiple different things on how to help him. That's when my family support specialist came in. My goal is to continue to help other families.

My son is more confident, and I've started to work again after two years of being at home. He's doing better in school and mentally growing... not only physically but mentally much more stable than before. It's not perfect, but I've learned how to create a safe environment for my son, and I'm not as afraid anymore, and I know how to ask for help.

Significance

OFSN is proud to help families grow and reach an optimal level of security within themselves and their communities. Many families have their own unique stories and journeys that OFSN has happily been a part of; whether their support has been long-term or short term their journey is equally important. But even as we work together with the families we support, it has been truly amazing to see how families have been able to reach new levels of growth, and it is so encouraging to hear how families are becoming bolder and more courageous in fighting for what they need.

To conclude and finalize these thoughts, as families are able to grow in skills, they shouldn't be made to feel like troublemakers because they are advocating for the needs of their family within the system.

Possible Responses

Adjustments

- Go into different regions and connect with community partners who are engaged with system change and learn about our supports and advocate and champion our work within their section of the system.

New Strategies

- Support families in telling their stories at system of care meetings/ Ways and Means committee
- Being intentional about system change as an opportunity for systemic growth and change.
- Increase the amount of trainings on empowerment/self-advocacy

Experiments

- Collaborative Problem Solving cohorts for families (Small groups for 3-6 months).
- Creating goals with the family with small action steps to achieve.

Finding 3: Into Me You See

Key Insight: Families are authentically known by each other and the staff of OFSN.

As a statewide organization, Oregon Family Support Network is able to reach all corners of communities within the state and provide support and resources to parents and caregivers for their families. This mission has expanded in our families, who are now truly "seeing" and connecting with each other as well. Throughout most of the interviews, parents and caregivers identified that through their engagement with OFSN, they were able to know their children more thoroughly and felt a true sense of love and appreciation for each other. One interviewee stated:

We aren't going to talk behind his back, no. It's [that] "he is an amazing kid, and he has issues, but you need to hear him," and we have more of a respect than before. It's a beautiful relationship, and I can truly say, "He loves me, and I love him," and he knows we value him.

Most parents and caregivers stated that their children were now able to express themselves more freely and openly, as parents and caregivers took more time to engage in active listening practices to understand what their children were saying rather than what they wanted to hear. This is what one interviewee stated:

I was raised to not talk as a child, so I made my kids do that too. Now, through CPS [Collaborative Problem Solving] classes, I have learned to really listen. That my kids have something important to say, and it's probably not what I think it is.

Many interviewees shared they felt they knew their children better, and they felt more known and accepted within their family unit as well. Although when we asked survey respondents if they felt their self-acceptance had increased, there was a somewhat lower than expected response, with 12% of respondents answering "very much" (see Figure 3). Nevertheless, the overall percentage of respondents indicating a positive change between the top three responses of "very much," "quite a bit" and "somewhat" was very encouraging to see and definitely seems to have validated what we uncovered in our interviews with families. But for those who had answered that there had been no change in their self-acceptance, this will give us a great launching point to help us to dive into a deeper level of support within OFSN to better reach those individuals and families.

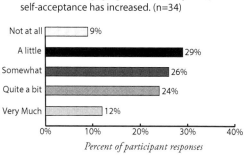

Figure 3. Since engaging with OFSN, my self-acceptance has increased. (n=34)

Percent of participant responses

An additional observation that we made during our interviews and analysis was how much more aware parents and caregivers were about ensuring their providers knew who their family was and how to help them. During an interview, one participant shared, "I learned how to talk in a way that other providers could understand while also ensuring that I wasn't giving away what we needed in the process."

Other participants stated similar comments, saying that they knew themselves and their families better and were able to determine when a plan would or would not be helpful. Another participant said, "I know what my kids and I need. Maybe not the exact treatment but at least a good idea."

Overall, it appears that parents and caregivers felt an increase in feeling and being known after working with OFSN. However, it seems that some of our survey data were somewhat divided on this. One question where we asked respondents about that same sense of belonging in their communities was met with some surprising results. Thirty-five percent of respondents reported there had been no change, with as little as 15% noting that they had experienced significant change for the better. Of course, this could be due to a variety of factors, for instance, maybe pointing to a feeling of belonging in their neighborhoods, churches, or districts and not necessarily in dealing with the support that OFSN has specifically been a part of with these families in helping them feel known and accepted. That said, further inquiry would definitely help to shed light on this matter and give us a clearer picture.

Significance

It has truly been illuminating to see the difference that is being made while families are making connections within their own family unit as well as in their communities. Regardless, we have been able to see for ourselves how much of an impact is happening when families are feeling truly connected. It seems that it has helped in ways that relate not only to emotional well-being but also how families are able to determine what programs would be most helpful and those that may do more harm than good.

Of course, there are concerns here as well, which have been revealed through our survey data, as many families have reported feeling a lack of connectedness and being known and seen in their communities. The last thing we want to do is make them feel less connected within their communities if there is an area that we are overlooking. This context will surely allow us to better reach our families, more so in areas that they need.

Possible Responses

Adjustments

- Strive to increase the number of families who feel accepted in their community from 35% to 100%

New Strategies

- Provide more opportunities for families to give feedback on working and navigating through the system.
- Create more culturally matching support groups for families
- focusing our work on cultivating champions within our communities to value and include family voice and choice at all levels.

Experiments

- Cultivating champions for family's voice and choice across systems by offering listening sessions to aid them in feeling more validated and connected to those around them.
- Increasing our relationship with more diverse communities to understand their needs.

Finding 4: Slowest Process of my Life! #Barriers

Key Insight: Families expressed discouragement with system processes.

Throughout our interviews, a deep sense of discouragement began surfacing. One major component of this discouragement was how slow children serving systems are to change and improve. When asked how interviewees felt about accessing resources and supports in the community, they shared these thoughts:

I have to make sure others are doing what they are supposed to do. As I get older, sometimes I find myself not having much patience. Other times, I know this is going to take time but stay on top of it. It's hard sometimes because I do lose patience and want to give up.

That it never ends (barriers to services), and there is no easy way through it. They make it hard on purpose. They want people to give up because it's easier and cheaper for them.

There were many other parents and caregivers who also agreed with these statements, holding the belief that services and supports for families were often made challenging to access on purpose. This also held true within our survey responses, as over 50% of those respondents stated that they felt no sense of equity within the system.

Additionally, parents and caregivers shared financial barriers to accessing resources and supports. For instance, the burden of paying rent, expenses incurred from transportation services, and even medications were challenging for some families, which then was further compounded by the challenges families were facing in other capacities. This is what two interviewees shared on that topic:

We don't really make enough to live. We barely survive. OFSN has been great for helping with [food] boxes, but everything is so expensive. There is never enough.

The best [providers] are the most expensive, and [they] don't take OHP (Oregon Health Plan). Makes it impossible to actually get better because providers at a clinic are new and inexperienced.

The last area of discouragement that families discussed in our interviews were with providers. This ranged from the length of time it took to access real supports to experiencing distrust for professionals and their treatment options. One interviewee shared the following:

I was very let down by a professional expert. When he found out we were doing a certain thing, he wanted us to change and do a different thing. Threatened to turn us over to DHS if we didn't. Destroyed my trust in [the] medical field.

There were, unfortunately, quite a few instances where interviewees had shared similar experiences with providers. As we compared this to our survey data, we found that 47% of respondents reported that their frustration level in navigating systems even after working with OFSN had not decreased at all (see Figure 4).

Figure 4. Since working with OFSN, my frustration level in navigating systems is less. (n=34)

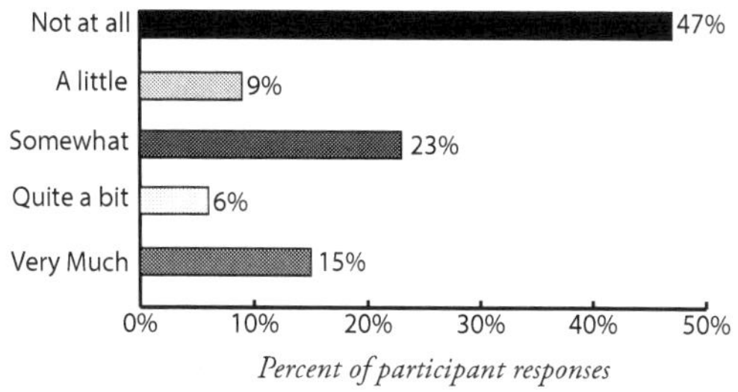

Percent of participant responses

Unfortunately, this leaves a wide rift between families and providers as there is an obvious lack of trust. One interviewee described how they experienced this discouragement, saying, "Every agency I worked with just saw me as a single parent with a kid with autism. They didn't want to know our story or experience, [or ask] why we needed their help." Another shared, "She ran late to meetings; I was never sure if she was actually going to show up to meet with me. It felt like my life was around her schedule."

Significance

While this has been one of our more shocking findings to discover, it has truly been insightful as we have learned that this experience of distrust and discouragement with providers can be so common. Moving forward, we will be able to use these insights to better reach the families we support. Perhaps more importantly, we will now be able to better understand the challenges and problems that families face and how we can advocate for them in the ways that they so desperately need. This context will not only offer OFSN an opportunity to improve its supports but ultimately improve relationships that service providers maintain with families.

Possible Responses

Adjustments

- Increase our provider network, so families get what they need when they need it.
- Community partners and providers to take a more holistic approach to the family rather than just considering the identified child or youth.

New Strategies

- Advocating at a system level.
- More follow-ups.
- Take a more holistic approach towards families, especially for those who are in recovery and experiencing crisis.

Experiments

- Participating in different child and youth meetings with community partners and providers to share the family experience.

Finding 5: Becoming an Agent of Change

Key Insight: Families supported by OFSN do not always understand how they can begin to work with our system partners and staff and how, through that involvement, it can become the catalyst to better impact internal change within the family.

Throughout a lot of our interviews that we conducted with families, we came to find that they did not always understand how they are able to work with system partners and other OFSN staff in order to better bring forth a more positive influence of change in their families. One mother, in particular, voiced that by the time they had come into communication with our staff, she had been doing a lot of work on her own to advocate for herself and her family, and as a result of that experience, she had a harder time having the capacity to understand and be educated about a new process.

This was something we saw confirmed in our survey findings as well, as 41% of participants answered "not at all" when asked if they recognize that their involvement within the system brings forth change. Whether that has resulted from a thread of discouragement, as seen in other interviews and data, remains to be seen. But a common thread seemed to be voiced in the comment made by some respondents who said, "I don't believe in mental health" or "I don't have the capacity for that."

Understandably, many other parents across our discussions spoke to a factor of time affecting this as well. They described that in the fast-paced nature of their lives that they simply did not have the time to dedicate themselves to a process to understand how their lived experiences can be used for a more intentional purpose in a way that would provide better advocacy for the family. This is what one mother said on that point,

> I would be more willing and able to reach out, but at times, life can get busy, and honestly, things can take a long time to get moving, which can also get pretty frustrating. I can't say that I like it, but there it is. Change is hard. You can say that patience will win out, but that's not always the case, at least all the time.

While this has been the experience with a good amount of the people that we interviewed, there was a small handful of others who spoke on coming to a better understanding as they became more involved in the process and in their communities. They have been able to create healthier family dynamics as their involvement with system partners and other OFSN staff has grown.

Similarly, in some of our survey data, we saw a somewhat encouraging response to validate this idea. Forty-seven percent of our respondents reported that they know how to better find resources and support for their families, having indicated a response of "Very Much or "Quite a Bit" to the statement: I now know how to find resources and support for my family (See Figure 5, next page). However, there is always more work to be done here, as there are still many families who we can continue to reach on this.

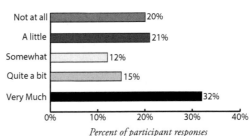

Figure 5. Through my engagement with OFSN, I now know how to find resources and support for my family. (n=34)

Percent of participant responses

Significance

This finding has been very insightful as we have been able to see where we can further impact more positive change for families. Unfortunately, it seems that many families have fallen by the wayside, as there appears to be a lot of confusion around this specific topic. It also seems apparent that we need to increase awareness with our system partners so that they know how to better connect families with the specific resources that they might need.

But learning more about the experiences that families have had and being able to see into their lives and gain a better understanding of what they are going through will allow us to connect them with specific programs and learning opportunities that are of particular importance and, more importantly, relevant to their specific circumstance.

Possible Responses

Adjustments

◆ Increase family awareness of their role in system change.

New Strategies

◆ Offering an increased amount of educational opportunities for mental and behavioral health for families.

Experiments

◆ Providing quarterly educational opportunities for families to increase their knowledge as it relates to the systems they are navigating

Finding 6: Building the Toolbox

Key Insight: Families supported by OFSN gain knowledge and practice new skills through training and classes.

It is evident that families being supported by OFSN were not only able to dial into a higher degree of knowledge but also gain a new skill set through training and classes. One mother specifically described how she had been able to grow in her communication skills throughout Collaborative Problem Solving (CPS) classes and other parenting programs and classes, saying, "I also took a CPS class, so that helped with understanding how to talk in a way that my kids would listen, without being walked all over."

One mother talked about training and classes focused on Trauma Informed Care, which teaches how to manage the stress of daily life as a single parent in a trauma-informed way that is not harmful to your sense of self or others. She shared simply, "That's something that everyone needs."

Being able to provide structure and stability seemed to be a key proponent of this, that with the access to those community resources, trainings and classes, parents have now been able to develop the skills in order to be more successful parents and caregivers in order to recognize their family's needs. This last point, specifically regarding recognition of needs, was one of the most encouraging results from our survey. Ninety-four percent of respondents reported that, at least on some level, there had been a positive increase, with only 6% stating there had been no change (See Figure 6).

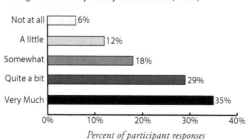

Figure 6. Through my engagement with OFSN, I am able to better recognize what my family's needs are. (n=34)

Percent of participant responses

While conducting the interviews, it was apparent that the classes and resources that have been offered to families have been able to instill a great many skills so that parents can work to create a more positive environment for their families to be a part of.

One mother further elaborated on this, saying that she felt she had a better understanding of community support, specifically with being able to lead her family in her role, and was now beginning to see increased capabilities in her children. Similarly, this is what one interviewee shared on that matter,

I knew where we are and who we are as well. I just needed to practice it more. I think I am less afraid, and so are my kids about the future and what we can do. I think we are more capable now than before because we are less afraid of what might happen. We are more trusting that we will be okay if it ends badly.

Significance

Being able to learn and advance yourself in new skills, some of which may feel so foreign at times, is truly one of the greatest gifts that we can give to families. It's not only that we are giving families access to resources that can help them in the short term, but in the long term as well, as that will ultimately be what causes the most sustainable impact on families. Even after they have left the care of OFSN, they will be able to continue to reach out for support and listen to their children's needs and be able to act on them in an effective manner.

Possible Responses

Adjustments

- ◆ Give greater access to resources that are specific to foster a good environment of growth for families as a whole.

New Strategies

- ◆ Begin to offer increased opportunities for families to share their personal experiences and their specific family needs.

Experiments
- Provide families with skill-building resources through workshops, online webinars, and training sessions
- Connecting families with other families who have had similar experiences.

Finding 7: Patience is a Virtue

Key Insight: Families supported by OFSN gain an increased capacity for patience with their families and the system.

A lot of the families that have been involved throughout the programs offered at OFSN shared that they had come to better understand and practice the skill of patience. Many families spoke individually about how they are able to recognize when they are starting to feel overwhelmed. They are able to take that situation and reframe it in such a way that they are now learning to be patient not only with themselves but also within their families. One particular mother commented on how she had learned to look at situations in a more positive light, saying,

There's always negative things that can happen. But there's also the positive to see...My kids are always trying to do the best that they can, and I know I'm not perfect, but what matters is that we're trying.

In many of these encounters, we noticed how families described that, at times, they struggle with learning to navigate the system. But what was interesting to hear is that even within those struggles that the families deal with, there has been such an amazing resolve to work through them. They are being patient with the systems and support agents that they work with in getting their needs met, even when that support doesn't always happen immediately. One example from our survey data that seemed to tie into this was how respondents have been better able to accept where their family is at in their journey. Only 9% reported they felt no change, which definitely seems to speak to how family dynamics are changing in this way (See Figure 7, next page).

Figure 7. After engaging with OFSN, I am more
accepting of my family's journey. (n=34)

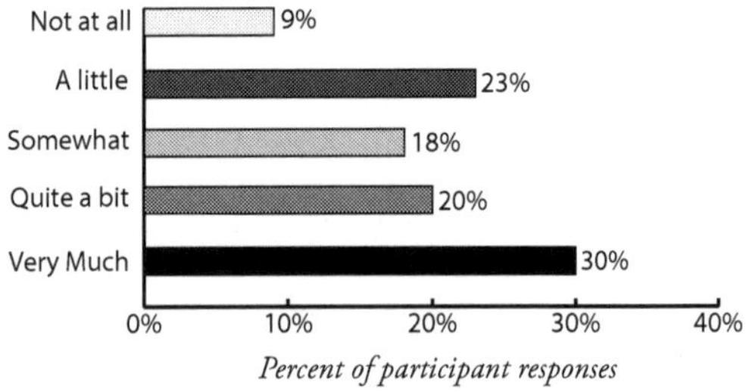

Response	Percent
Not at all	9%
A little	23%
Somewhat	18%
Quite a bit	20%
Very Much	30%

Percent of participant responses

Other interview participants further shared that as they are learning how to practice this skill, they are becoming more equipped to handle the conflicts that arise and are able to give themselves "grace" in order to take a step back and see that change is actually possible and that these things simply take time.

Significance

We think it can be proven that patience has the ability to transform relationships. These findings that we have discovered seem to illustrate this point as it seems that families are now better working together to overcome the obstacles that they face, and at the same time becoming accepting of where their family is at and having the patience to understand that. Being able to work through programs and systems that are at times difficult to navigate through and calmly wait for that breakthrough is not easy by any means. But we are now able to have a greater insight into what families experience daily and how we might be able to better step into a role that would allow us to further alleviate the frustration that families experience and give them more empathy.

Possible Responses

Adjustments

◆ Increasing the knowledge of system partners on the strength and resilience that families already have.

New Strategies

- Raising the awareness with system partners regarding who the families are that they are supporting.

Experiments

- Sharing family stories of resilience.

Finding 8: Hope on the Horizon

Key Insight: Families supported by OFSN experience an increased sense of hope for their families and their futures.

At Oregon Family Support Network, changing the perspectives of families from hopeless to hopeful is an important aspect of our vision. We were excited to hear that perspective change occurs for families during our interviews. One parent shared,

> *I couldn't have imagined my kids would be living in their home and not breaking windows and ruining walls. One of the twins went to residential for five months, and there was talk of her needing a longer placement. So, to see them thriving, other than school, is phenomenal. I think we have more capacity to do things and be normal people in the world.*

Many parents and caregivers during our interviews either stated or demonstrated new hope for their families. This included hope for the future and where their family is going, and, in some cases, where their family is at. As we have compared this to our survey data, we have also seen a positive response. When asked if they now have a clearer vision for their family's future, 42% of our respondents reported "very much" or "quite a bit" (See Figure 8, next page). Another 29% responded "somewhat." This is what a few of our interviewees had to say on the matter,

> *We are finally talking about seeing my parents, who I haven't visited in 10 years. The girls were always too unstable in new environments, but we are planning how to make that happen this summer.*

It's changed a lot (the family dynamics). I didn't know he was suffering the way he was. Through talks/interactions on a daily basis, it's opened my eyes. I think we are getting stronger as a whole.

Figure 8. After being supported by OFSN, I have a clearer vision of my family's future. (n=34)

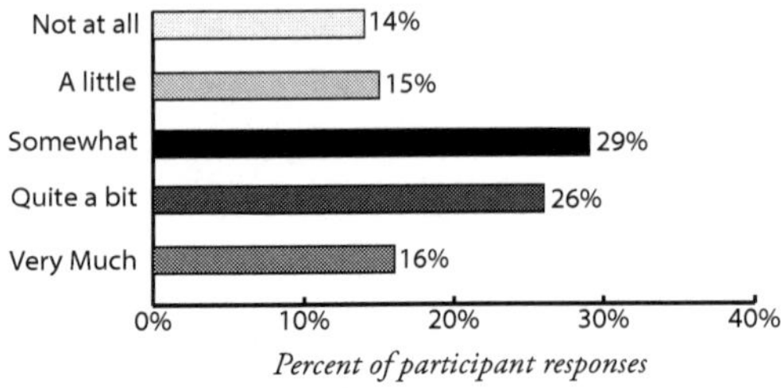

Percent of participant responses

To conclude, it was evident that when parents spoke about their experiences with their children, there was an increase in hope. This is what a few of our participants said as they elaborated more on their family's story,

I used to be so mad at [my son], but now I know he doesn't mean it (his behaviors). I can see past them and realize he just needs something that he doesn't have yet.

I think we have become more comfortable being adventurous and more willing to try new things. We got to go to a water park through the kids' school. Normally we wouldn't even think about it. The people, being exposed in our bathing suits, the water being unsanitary. But we tried it. It was hard, but we did it.

Significance

We have been greatly encouraged by this finding; to hear from these families on how they are gaining a vision for their families. There is almost nothing that can compare. It is vital in this work that OFSN completes with families that they gain this kind of hope and vision, as without it, how can there be goals to forecast what a family will be able to truly accomplish? While families had previously lived in a state of not being able to deviate from the status quo they had been set on for so long, now they have been able to step out in faith as it were to leave their comfort zones, to be adventurous, and even be able to experience a new vision for their family.

Moreover, it has also seemed apparent that when families are able to have this hope, they are better able to create a safe and perhaps even more enjoyable environment for their children that is conducive to their growth and development.

Possible Responses

Adjustments

- Having an expectation that system partners lead the work that they do with families in a strength-based person-first approach.

New Strategies

- Model the strength-based approach when working with system partners.

Experiments

- Sharing and identifying our strengths in our own lived experiences with system and community partners.

Conclusion

Insights Into Impact

As a result of our support offered to families through OFSN, we found that families have been able to express themselves authentically through their individual experience, culture, and worldview. Through the interviews and data collection that we had undergone, we have seen that families feel most empowered when they feel fully seen and known and that the potential for the greatest impact is made when those families are put into a position of being empowered where they can lead the charge with the types of support that they need and are ultimately the decision maker.

We have also found that families are finding the courage to speak their truth as they navigate challenging situations, and in doing so, they are acknowledged as experts of their lived experience. While it's true that a family finding their voice is something that we always encourage, it's also true that through this type of support, they will be able to better navigate youth and family serving systems with confidence. Through our interactions, we have seen that families know how to better access the support they feel they need, especially when they are involved in the decision-making.

Similarly, another aspect of our interaction has been that when families are fully known and seen, they are more hopeful and confident about their circumstances and also their future. One of the goals that we consistently work towards has been intentionally looking for areas of strength and hope and gifting those back to the family so they can see that hope returned back to them.

Lastly, when families are coming out of isolation and they're building a sense of community with other families who have endured similar experiences, they feel better supported and find a sense of belonging. Even through the support groups and other services that families have access to, they are able to build those natural supports outside of service providers to further empower themselves.

Steps Forward

To continue in the work that we do in supporting families who are facing challenging situations and to help empower them in the ways that they most need, OFSN would like to implement the following steps into our policies and trainings to improve and bridge those gaps that families encounter in daily life.

Several examples of these include:

1. **Reach out deeper into communities to understand their needs.** We found through our interviews that we do need to reach deeper into the communities to truly understand a family's needs better. The more we know about families, and also com-

munities that are culturally specific, the more we will be able to better support them.

2. **Go into different regions and connect with community partners who are engaged with system change.** We found that families don't always know how their voice and experiences can impact the system through their advocacy, and so a step forward for us will be to find those opportunities to go out into the community and partner with families so they can better learn and understand about our supports and be able to advocate and champion themselves within their section of the system.

3. **Creating goals with the family with small action steps to achieve.** Another example that we would like to further pursue with our families is to work with them to create these goals with small action steps that are within their power to achieve. While in this process, we also hope to validate their experiences and let them know it's okay that they don't have to have everything together all at once.

Opportunities for Future Evaluation

We are beyond excited to apply the techniques and methodologies learned here to be able to further investigate the impacts that are being made on the families and the communities that we support. Moving forward, OFSN plans to conduct interviews with families that not only capture hard, quantifiable data but also the experiences that we will only truly gain insight into by speaking with the families that we serve personally.

Our goal and plan is to do a series of presentations with all our findings, introducing these concepts to our board of directors so that they may see the impacts that are being made with the families that we support and also so that we can expand on these ideas in future evaluations to reach a wider range of families and communities.

Appendix

Oregon Community Programs Qualitative Interview Protocol
What have you noticed or come to recognize about how the TFCO model differs from traditional foster parent care? → How has this made you think differently about the value of a team-based approach to foster care? (Know/Believe)

What new treatment foster care skills have you developed as a result of the program? Which of the skills have been the most challenging to master? Where have you found yourself getting stuck? v What is your process for working through those moments? (Do/Become)

What new habits did you develop as a result of group participation? What habits have you had to unlearn? → How have you been modeling these changes to newer foster parents? (Do/Become)

What have you come to better understand about the essential foster parenting elements during your participation in this program? What still feels confusing or difficult to understand? → How has this changed the way you view your role as a TFCO foster parent? In what ways have your assumptions been challenged? (Know/Believe)

What have you learned about setting goals and focusing on long-term gains with the foster youth in your home? → How has this shifted your perceptions around what foster youth are capable of accomplishing? (Know/Believe)

Through your interaction with OCP, how has your confidence in your ability as a foster parent changed? → How are you more determined to foster long-term change in the youth living with you? (Feel/Love)

What actions have you taken to get the support you need when it gets challenging to continue as a TFC parent? → How have you adapted in order to navigate those challenges? What needs to further develop and grow in you to be able to continue in the foster parent role? (Do/Become)

What still concerns you about continuing to work with challenging kids? → How does this impact your commitment to being a long-term foster parent? (Feel/Love)

What is most energizing (rewarding?) to you about being a foster parent? → How has this shaped your commitment to the treatment foster parent model? (Feel/Love)

Looking ahead 3-5 years, if everything goes as well as it possibly could, what does the future look like for you and the kids who live with you? What is your vision for what is possible for you and for them?

Be Your Best Qualitative Interview Protocol
What excites you about working in collaboration? What feels rewarding? → Describe what keeps you engaged with Be Your Best and the work? How have you cultivated/nourished your relationships with community partners? (Feel → Love)

What have you discovered about your role in the community through your involvement with Be Your Best? What have you noticed about how you relate/communicate with other partners? → How has this served to shift your way of seeing challenges and opportunities? (Know → Believe)

What do you try to do now that you weren't doing before you joined Be Your Best? What habits have you had to unlearn? What do you wish you could do that you haven't done yet? → How has this affected how you show up as a community advocate and on behalf of others? What needs to grow and develop in you to continue this work? (Do → Become)

What are some of the key learnings you have gained since you've been involved with Be Your Best? What feels hard to understand or is confusing? What has been most helpful? → How has this changed your perspective of the community? How have your assumptions been challenged? (Know → Believe)

What have you been experimenting with that resulted from your involvement with Be Your Best? What have you tried that has not worked? → How have you integrated these into your approach to work and relationships? (Do → Become)

What feels difficult or frustrating about working in collaboration? What drives you crazy? → What keeps you committed to this effort? How do you push through frustration when things get challenging? (Feel → Love)

During your time with Be Your Best, what have you learned about assessing impact? → How is that evolving your view of yourself and your capabilities? What about for your organization? (Know → Believe)

What new practices has your organization tried out around assessing your impact since you've been with Be Your Best? → How has this changed the way you approach your work? (Do → Become)

How are you more energized about the potential for the community since you've been involved with Be Your Best? What feels deflating? What are you still anxious about? → How has this affected your values and passions around your commitment to community work and collaboration? What kind of values and passions will need to be forged in all of us to make this a reality and to overcome despair? (Feel → Love)

Final Question: What are you most hopeful for? For your organization? For our community?

Burrito Brigade Qualitative Interview Protocol

What have you noticed or observed about your experiences shopping at Waste to Taste? What has been most surprising or eye opening? → How/ In what ways has this led you to think differently about your connection to food and your community? (Know/Believe)

What has changed about your family's way of eating as a result of your participation in Waste to Taste? → How has your family's relationship with food evolved or changed because of that? (Do/Become)

What does your family/household do now (related to food, meals, cooking, well-being) that you didn't do before as a result of Waste to Taste? What has your family been most excited or enthusiastic to try? → What have you and your family cherished most about meal times since shopping at Waste to Taste? Can you identify some "feel good" moments or occasions? (Feel/Love)

What food choices do you make at Waste to Taste that you might not have made previously? What have you been wanting to try but haven't yet? → How has this affected the role that food plays in your household? (Do/Become)

What ways has your household budget been stretched because of Waste to Taste? → How/In what ways has this affected your beliefs about your household's financial outlook/future? (Know/Believe)

What has your family been able to accomplish (or do) within your household budget that you couldn't do before coming to Waste to Taste? What do you wish you could do that you haven't done yet? How has this impacted the way you live your day-to-day life? (Do/Become)

What do you still find frustrating about procuring food for you and your family? → How/In what ways could these burdens be lessened? → What keeps you committed to maintaining agency/independence/control over your family's food choices or way of eating? (Feel/Love)

What do you know now about food waste that you didn't know before you shopped at Waste to Taste? What has been most surprising to you? What still feels confusing or difficult to understand? → How/In what ways do you see yourself/your family as part of the solution to reducing food waste? (Know/Believe)

What most energizes you about your family's future as a result of Waste to Taste? What still worries you or makes you anxious? → How has being able to get food from Waste to Taste helped shape your hopes for your family's future? (Feel/Love)

Oregon Family Support Network Qualitative Interview Protocol

What have you discovered about yourself while working with OFSN? What has been most surprising to see in yourself? → How do you see yourself differently now as a parent/caregiver? How have those affected your values and beliefs about yourself and your family? (Know/Believe)

What steps have you taken during your interaction with OFSN to work toward the vision you have for yourself and your family? Where do you still feel stuck, like you aren't making progress? → What needs to continue to develop inside of you to make this vision a reality? What continues to hold you back? (Do/Become)

While receiving services at OFSN, what skills have you implemented to ensure your needs are being met? What sort of things still feel challenging that you would like to be able to do? → How do you show up differently now for your family because of these skills? What changes have others noticed and commented on? (Do/Become)

What have you come to better understand about your family during your support with OFSN? → How has your perception of your story changed because of this? How has this changed the way you think about your family's capabilities? (Know/Believe)

What fears or insecurities affected your ability to feel comfortable with all aspects of yourself and your family? How have these changed through your time with OFSN? → In what ways are you more settled and centered than before? (Feel/Love)

Through your engagement with OFSN, how has your confidence level shifted when attempting to access resources and support for your family? What is still frustrating to you? → How has that affected your commitment to systemic change? (Feel/Love)

What have you learned about navigating system challenges? What still feels confusing? → How has the way you perceive challenges changed? (Know/Believe)

What has been the most rewarding part of your experience with OFSN? What has been the most difficult? → What has it meant to you and your family to be a part of this? (Feel/Love)

What accomplishments have you achieved as a family through your time with OFSN? What do you wish you could do that you haven't done yet? What's holding you back? → How have you grown as individuals and as a family during this time? (Do/Become)

Made in the USA
Las Vegas, NV
26 April 2023

71142674R00066